creative glass

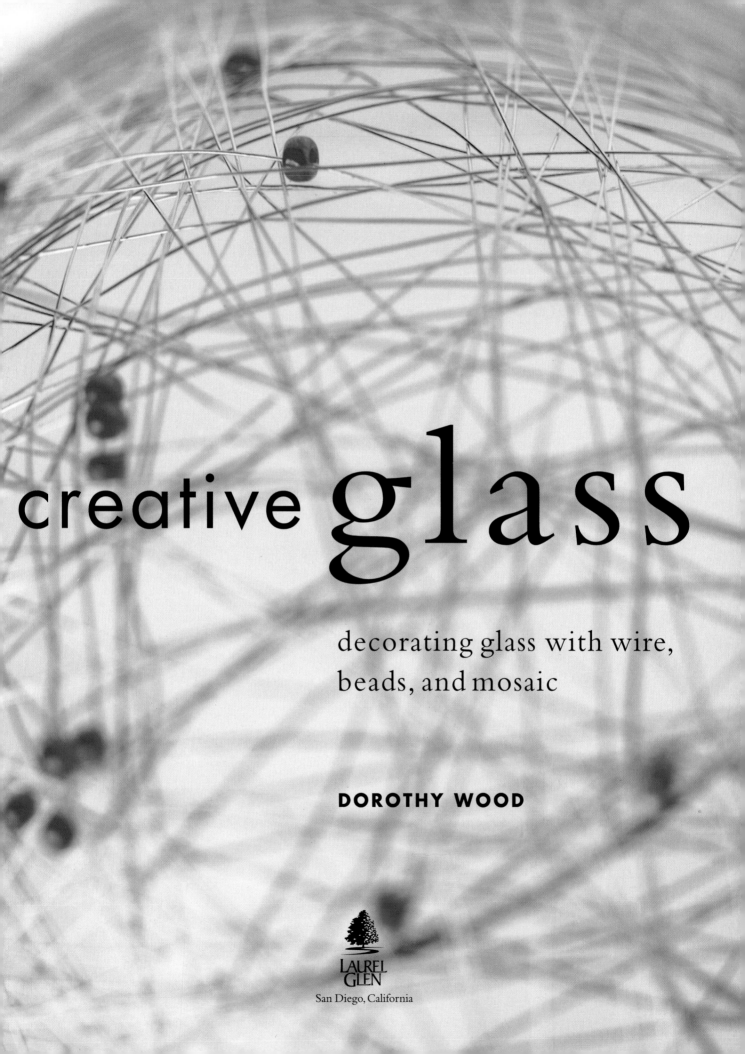

creative glass

decorating glass with wire, beads, and mosaic

DOROTHY WOOD

LAUREL
GLEN

San Diego, California

Laurel Glen Publishing
An imprint of the Advantage Publishers Group
5880 Oberlin Drive, San Diego, CA 92121-4794
www.advantagebooksonline.com

ISBN 1-57145-816-6
Library of Congress Cataloging-in-Publication Data available upon
request.

Printed in Malaysia
1 2 3 4 5 06 05 04 03 02

Senior Editor: CLARE JOHNSON
Editor: CLAIRE WAITE
Production: HAZEL KIRKMAN
Design: LISA TAI
Photographer: JOHN FREEMAN
Editorial Direction: ROSEMARY WILKINSON

NOTE
The author and publishers have made every effort to ensure that all
instructions given in this book are safe and accurate, but they
cannot accept liability for any resulting injury or loss or damage to
either property or person, whether direct or consequential and to
whatever degree or extent.

contents

introduction

A plain piece of glass is like a blank artist's canvas, waiting to be embellished and transformed into a beautiful object. Buying a simple object made from clear glass and seeing it come to life with the added color and texture of wire, beads, or mosaic is such an exciting process. The beauty of this type of decoration is that you don't need any particular artistic skill. If you are good with your hands, are comfortable using basic tools like pliers and wire cutters, and enjoy a challenge, you should have no problems at all.

This book includes a wide range of designs that are suitable for people of all abilities. With just a few basic tools, you can begin many of these projects immediately. The stunningly simple vase on pages 30–32 or the pretty pitcher on pages 52–55 are suitable for absolute beginners, and there are more advanced projects, such as the wire basket on pages 22–26 and the mosaic rectangular vase on pages 72–75, for those with more experience in working with wire and mosaic tiles.

There are so many different types of glassware that you can decorate that the possibilities are endless. Each piece can be embellished in a variety of ways. However, you may find that although a glass object's shape is inspiring, it can also restrict your choice. For example, the mosaic technique is much easier to execute on a flat surface or shallow curve, and wire needs something to attach itself to or be supported by, such as the shape of the object. Beads can be stuck directly onto glass or held in place with wire or a wire mesh. Whatever the shape and size of your piece of glass, you will find something of a similar style in this book and will be able to adapt the technique used to decorate it to make your own unique design.

left: wineglasses, bowls, vases, tumblers, oven dishes, pitchers, and decanters are just some of the glass objects that can be decorated with wire, beads, or mosaic tiles.

materials

The materials used to decorate the pieces of glass in this book are available from hardware and craft stores, although mail-order companies can supply anything that you can't find locally.

Galvanized wire is used by florists, gardeners, and model makers, so you should be able to find it in garden centers or from craft suppliers. Silver, gold, copper, and brass wires are used for jewelry making, so a range can be found in larger craft stores or from specialty suppliers. Wire thickness is measured by its gauge—the higher the gauge, the thinner the wire.

You may need to use a mail-order supplier for some of the less common thicknesses.

Unless you are lucky enough to live near a bead shop, the easiest way to buy beads of all shapes and sizes is by mail-order catalog or on the Internet. Many bead companies have their own websites where you can order a catalog or browse through the wonderful ranges of beads and buy online.

Mosaic tesserae and ceramic and vitreous glass tiles are sold in most craft stores, as well as in some hardware stores.

Aluminum wire

Aluminum wire is soft and pliable, and one of the easiest wires to use. It has a dull gray finish that doesn't rust and can be polished with a metal cleaner. Avoid using it with serrated pliers, since these will damage its surface. Aluminum wire is available from electrical suppliers or hardware stores.

Enameled copper wire

This wire is primarily used in the electronics industry, but comes in such a wide range of colors that it is ideal for wirework. Most craft stores sell enameled copper wire, but for a full range of colors and thicknesses, try a mail-order supplier.

Galvanized wire

Galvanized wire is steel wire with zinc coating that keeps it from rusting, making it ideal for outdoor use. Heavyweight galvanized wire is sold in large coils for modeling, and florists stock straight lengths in several thinner gauges.

Jewelry wire

Brass, copper, silver, and gold wires are most commonly used for jewelry making. The wire can be pure metal, mixed with another metal, or plate, and is available in a range of gauges from bead suppliers and craft stores.

Wire mesh

Wire mesh is available in sheets or rolls from hardware stores or craft suppliers. It is most commonly made from aluminum, but brass and galvanized wire mesh are also available. The mesh is made in different gauges with grid holes of various shapes and sizes, from the finest, for filters, to heavyweight chicken wire.

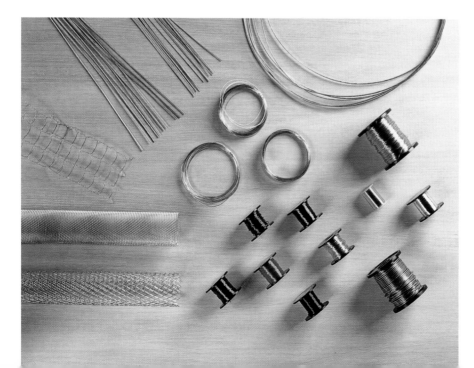

left: a selection of different types of wire and wire mesh.

Wire-mesh ribbon

Wire-mesh ribbon is a new material available from selected florists. It comes in a range of widths. You can make your own mesh by knitting or crocheting fine wire.

Beads

Beads are made from a huge range of different materials and are available in various sizes, from the tiny seed beads used for embroidery to large beads usually seen on chunky jewelry. General craft suppliers will stock some beads, but for the widest range, refer to a mail-order company.

Crimps

Crimps are tiny metal rings that are used to hold beads in position on a length of wire. Gold and silver are the most common colors and are available from craft stores.

above: beads are made from a range of different materials, from ceramic to glass.

Mosaic tesserae

There are lots of different materials that can be used for mosaic, such as pebbles or broken china, but most people use specially made tesserae that are of an even thickness, easy to use, and available from craft stores. Unglazed ceramic tesserae are the easiest tiles to use because they can be cut very simply and accurately. They are generally made in muted, earthy colors and are 1 in. square. Vitreous glass tesserae feature the widest range of bright colors and are ideal for decorative work. They can be translucent, opaque, or even striated with metallic ores. The most common tiles are ¾ in. square, but smaller ½-in. tiles are also available, reducing the need for cutting in many instances.

left: ready-made tesserae come in a range of materials and sizes.

equipment

With all tools, it is advisable to buy the best you can afford. A good-quality tool will work well, last longer, and give a more professional result for your efforts. It is also important, especially when working with materials such as wire and mosaic tesserae, that you use the recommended safety equipment.

Drill and cup hook

Depending on the weight of the wire, you can use either an electric or a hand drill. Jewelry wire is easy to twist with a lightweight drill, but galvanized wire requires a stronger tool. A cup hook is the easiest way to attach the wire and is simply fitted into the chuck.

Masking tape

This is a low-tack tape that is used to hold work in position temporarily. For a stronger adhesion, use clear tape.

Mosaic equipment

Mosaic equipment is available from craft stores and from large hardware stores.

Glass cutters are pliers with a glass cutter on the underside. They are used to make triangles or thin strips from mosaic tiles. A straight line is scored on the top surface of the tile and then the jaws are used to break the tile along that line.

Mosaic **tile nippers** have the jaws set to one side and can be used to cut glass and ceramic mosaic tiles. The jaws are straight on one side and curved on the other. Buy a pair with a spring between the handles so that the jaws open again after each cut.

Strong **white school glue** dries clear and is ideal for sticking both glass and ceramic tiles to glass objects. Leave the glued mosaic for twenty-four hours before finishing with a **powdered grout** made for mosaic. You can add **watercolor paint** to grout to change its color.

Use a **grout spreader** or the back of a spoon to apply the grout and wipe off the excess from the surface with a **sponge**. A ⅛-in. notched squeegee can also be used to apply grout or the **cement-based adhesive** used when white school glue is not sufficient.

Paper and pens

Layout paper is thin enough to see through, but easier to handle than tracing paper. It is useful for altering the placement of motifs to fit the pattern template of a particular project. Use a medium **marker pen** to draw out templates. Ordinary pencils and pens do not work well on glass, so use a felt-tip **overhead projector pen** instead.

Pliers

Flat-nosed pliers come in a range of sizes and have serrated jaws to grip wire. However, on softer wires, such as aluminum, the serrations can leave unsightly marks. **Parallel pliers**, which have jaws that close parallel to one another, have smooth jaws that won't damage the surface of the wire. They grip well because the wire is held equally along its length. Use these pliers to bend and straighten wire. **Round-nosed pliers** are used to create small rings at the end of a length of wire and to make coils of wire. The jaws are graduated to create a range of ring sizes.

Safety equipment

A **dust mask** will keep you from breathing in the glass particles or dust thrown up each time you cut a mosaic tile. If you inhale this dust over long periods of time, it will eventually damage your lungs.

Protective gloves can be useful for different tasks. Wear heavy **gardening gloves** when cutting and working with wire mesh and thin **latex gloves** when applying grout, which is very drying for the skin and also a potential allergen.

When cutting wire or mosaic tiles, wear **safety glasses** to protect yourself from shattering glass or ceramic, or from the end of the wire, which can spring up and hit your face. Glasses with reinforced plastic lenses should provide sufficient protection.

Soldering iron, solder, and flux

Solder and **flux** are used together and heated with a **soldering iron** to join two pieces of metal together permanently. They are usually available from electrical suppliers, but liquid safety flux and 50:50 tin/lead solder, sold by stained-glass suppliers, is less expensive and easy to use. Electrical solder that has the flux built in works just as well, but can be expensive.

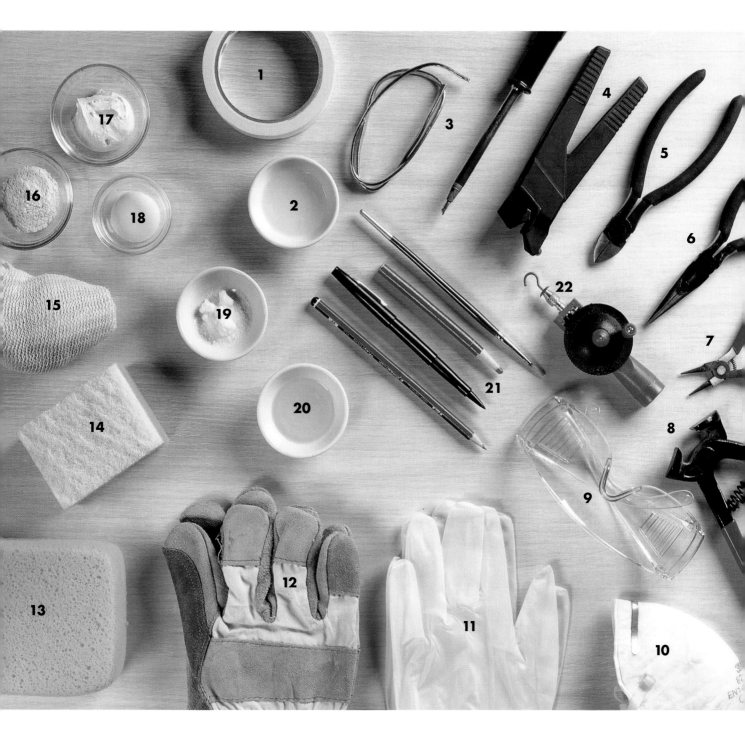

Wire cutters

Although most pliers have jaws for cutting wire, **wire cutters** are much easier to use when trimming the ends of wires on an actual project. Wire cutters have hardened, tempered steel jaws and are available in various sizes. Small pairs do look very neat, but cutters with long handles have better leverage for cutting galvanized wire.

above: much of the equipment used for the projects in this book is basic, but some you will have to buy from specialty stores.

1	masking tape	**6**	flat-nosed pliers
2	flux	**7**	round-nosed
3	solder and		pliers
	soldering iron	**8**	tile nippers
4	glass cutter	**9**	safety glasses
5	wire cutters	**10**	dust mask

11	latex gloves
12	gardening gloves
13	sponge
14	scourer
15	soft cloth
16	powdered grout
17	ready-made tile adhesive

18	white school glue
19	ammonia salt
20	copper patina
21	paintbrushes, pens, and pencils
22	hand drill and cup hook

basic techniques

wirework

Wire is a wonderfully versatile material that can be bent, coiled, twisted, spiraled, and woven to make innumerable different textures and shapes. There are lots of wirework techniques, and different ideas can be developed after learning the basics.

The two characteristics that make up different wires are the type of metal used and its thickness. The type of metal gives the wire its pliability and color, although plating or enameling can alter this. The thickness of wire is measured by the gauge. The higher the gauge, the thinner the wire.

BASIC WRAPPING

Basic wrapping adds color and texture to a plain wire and makes the wire more substantial. Use two wires of similar thickness, but make sure the outer wrapping wire is softer and more pliable than the core wire. Copper wire is one of the most suitable wires for wrapping, as it is soft and fairly inexpensive.

Close wrapping

● Wearing safety glasses, cut the core wire to the required length, allowing an extra 2 in. to form a winding loop. Using round-nosed pliers, make a loop at one end of the core wire. Twist one end of the wrapping wire around the loop.

● Wind the wrapping wire around the core wire at an angle. Keep the wraps close together to completely cover the core.

● To completely cover a particularly hard core wire, it can be easier to turn the core wire instead of the wrapping wire. Insert a pencil into the loop and use it as a winding mechanism (**1**). Use the finger and thumb of your other hand to keep the wrapping wire closely wrapped.

● When wrapping with a reel of wire, insert a long stick through the reel and hold the ends under your feet. This keeps the wrapping wire taut as you wind onto the core wire.

Loose wrapping

● Wearing safety glasses, cut the core wire to the required length, allowing an extra 2 in. to form a winding loop. Using round-nosed pliers, make a loop at one end of the core wire. Twist one end of the wrapping wire around the loop to secure it.

● Wind the wrapping wire around the core wire at an angle, leaving a small space between each wrap so that the core is still visible (**2**). Keep the wrapping wire at the same angle and the spacing between the wraps will remain the same along the full length of the core wire.

COILING

Both open and closed coils are used extensively in wirework. Coils are not only decorative, but they also neaten sharp ends of wire attractively. Invest in a pair of parallel pliers to make coils, as they keep the wire from being damaged.

Closed coil

● Using round-nosed pliers, make a small loop at the end of the wire. Hold the loop securely in the jaws of the pliers and wind the wire around once more so that the second circle of the coil almost touches the first loop.

● Now hold the ring with flat-nosed pliers and wind the wire around again. Keep

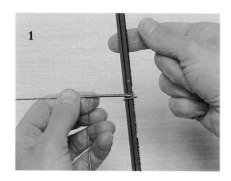

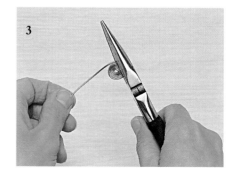

moving the coil around as you wind the wire until the coil is the required size (**3**).

Open coil

● Using round-nosed pliers, make a small loop at the end of the wire. Holding the loop securely in the pliers, bend the wire over your thumb to curve it around.

● Keep bending the wire gently to begin forming an open coil. Once the coil is a little larger, use parallel pliers to hold it in place as you continue bending the wire (**4**). Move the coil around as you wind the wire until the coil is the required size.

SPRINGS

Springs are made in a similar way to basic wrapping, except that the "core" is removed to leave a wire spring.

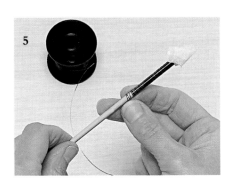

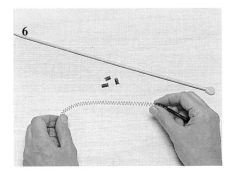

● Secure the wrapping wire at the end of the core implement with masking tape. Closely wrap the wire around the core (**5**).

● Slide the closely wrapped wire off the core. The spring can be cut into smaller lengths—wear safety glasses to do this—or pulled to make a curly, textured wire (**6**).

TWISTING

Twisting makes a wire stronger and adds texture. You can use two or more wires of different thicknesses and colors or simply fold a piece of wire in half and twist it. You can twist wires by hand, but for a more even twist, use a hand or electric drill. Most electric drills have two speeds; select the slower speed to twist the wire. Fine, soft wire can be twisted indoors using a small hand drill, but you will need a workbench and vise to twist galvanized wire.

● Wearing safety glasses, cut a piece of wire about two and a half times the required length. Fold it in half and secure the cut ends together with masking tape. Fit the taped ends securely in a vise.

● Insert a cup hook attachment into the chuck of the drill. Loop the folded wire over the hook and walk back until the wire is slightly taut.

● Wearing safety glasses again—in case the wire snaps—and with the drill set on a slow speed, twist the wire until the required degree of twist is reached (**7**). Switch the drill to reverse and wind in the other direction for a few seconds to release the tension before unhooking.

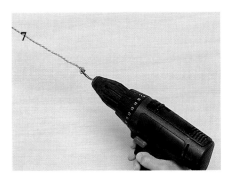

WEAVING

Basket techniques can be used quite successfully in wirework, using a pliable wire to weave over a harder structural wire. Enameled copper wire is ideal for weaving.

Plain weaving

● Create the basic basket structure with an odd number of uprights, equally spaced apart and bent into a flat star shape.

● Twist the weaving wire around the base of one of the uprights to secure it. Weave over and under the struts to create the basketwork (**8**).

Ribbed weaving

● Create the basic basket structure with any number of uprights, equally spaced apart and bent into a flat star shape.

● Twist the weaving wire around the base of one of the uprights to secure it. Wind the weaving wire around each upright before moving on to the next (**9**). Depending on which way you wind, you can either have ribs going up the outside of the basket or have a smooth surface with the ribs to the inside.

beadwork

Beads are available in all shapes and sizes, made from natural or man-made materials, and are one of the most versatile decorative items used in craftwork. You can buy beads from specialty bead stores or recycle old necklaces found in bric-a-brac stores. Beads add both color and texture to a piece of glass. Flat beads and cabochons can be glued directly onto the glass, while round beads are threaded onto wire or mesh before being secured to the glass.

CRIMPING

This simple technique holds beads in place on a wire.

● Thread a crimp onto the wire and then add the beads in the preferred order, finishing with a second crimp.

● Hold the beads in position on the wire and use flat-nosed pliers to squeeze the first crimp at one end.

● Let the beads fall down onto the fixed crimp and the second crimp fall onto the

beads. Squeeze the second crimp to secure the beads between the two (**1**).

SECURING BEADS TO WIRE MESH

Beads can be used to decorate wire mesh, positioned in a horizontal, vertical, or diagonal pattern.

Seed beads

● Tie some fine wire to the edge of the wire mesh. Thread the wire under the mesh bar, then thread on a bead and wrap the wire back under the same bar. Working either horizontally, vertically, or diagonally, add a bead to every bar (**2**).

● To add another length of wire, twist together the end of the new wire and the end of the previous wire, as close to the back of the bead as possible. Trim the ends and tuck out of sight behind the bead.

Ring beads

● Tie some fine wire to the edge of the wire mesh. Thread a bead onto the wire and take the wire under the mesh bar and back out through the hole in the bead. You can work either horizontally, vertically, or diagonally, adding a bead to every bar (**3**).

● If the mesh is shaped to fit the container, you may need to alter the spacing of the beads. If the beads start to touch one another, attach a bead to every second bar on the next row.

SECURING BEADS WITH WIRE

Beads can be threaded onto a thin wire—the wrapping wire—that is then twisted around a core wire so that the beads are held securely in a particular position. You can use just one method or mix the techniques along one length of wire to create interesting effects.

Basic wrapping

● Use round-nosed pliers to make a loop at the end of the core wire. Twist the end of a thinner wire around the loop to secure it and thread the required number of beads onto it.

● Wrap the thin wire around the core wire, trapping one bead at a time onto the core wire (**4**). The beads can be secured close together or spaced apart.

Stem

● To make the beads stand away from the core wire, use round-nosed pliers to make a loop at the end of the core wire and closely wrap with a thinner wrapping wire for a few inches (see Basic Wrapping, page 12).

● Pull the wrapping wire out to the side and thread on a bead. Fold the wrapping wire back on itself with the bead at the bend. Wrap the other end around the core wire once or twice. Hold the bead between your finger and thumb and twist so that the bent wrapping wire winds back around itself to create a stem. Continue to wrap the thinner wire

around the core wire and pull it out to create more stems as needed (**5**).

● To make a ring of beads, thread several beads onto the wrapping wire and fold the wire back on itself. Hold the beads between your finger and thumb and twist to create a stem.

Stem cluster

● To make a long cluster of beads stand out from the core wire, use round-nosed pliers to make a loop at the end of the core wire and closely wrap with a thinner wrapping wire for a few inches (see Basic Wrapping, page 12).

● Pull the wrapping wire out to the side and thread on the required number of beads for a single cluster, finishing with a seed bead. Leaving the seed bead, thread the wire back down through the other beads and pull taut so the cluster is held firmly in place. Continue to wrap the thinner wire around the core wire (**6**).

mosaic

Mosaic tiles can usually be fixed directly onto a glass surface, with small gaps between them that are filled with grout for a traditional look. The tiles can be used whole, but to depict specific shapes, such as petals and leaves, they will need to be individually cut.

CUTTING TECHNIQUES

Cutting is not difficult if you use the right tools and learn the basic techniques. There is no need for absolute accuracy in cutting mosaic tiles; it is more important to concentrate on the layout of the tiles and color choice on the overall design. Nevertheless, learning the correct technique is important and understanding how particular tiles break will help you to create the right shape for your design.

Wear safety glasses and a dust mask when cutting any mosaic material and work over a tray to catch any flying shards. Do not sweep the shards up with your hand, but tip the tray into the trash can or sweep up with a soft brush and dustpan.

Cutting rectangles and squares

● Mosaic tiles are often cut into quarters to make a smaller basic unit. Ceramic tesserae are the easiest to cut. Hold a ceramic tile firmly in one hand and place the flat side of the tile nippers on the edge of the tile, at a ninety-degree angle to it. Squeeze gently. The tile should break neatly across where the top of the cutter was positioned (**1**).

● Cut vitreous glass tesserae with tile nippers in the same way. On subsequent cuts, line up the nippers on the side of the tile that is not tapered at the edges (**2**).

● Cut rectangles in half in the same way to make four smaller squares (**3**). If the pieces are not very square, you are not holding the tile nippers at a ninety-degree angle to the tile.

● To make smaller rectangles, cut each of the small squares in three (**4**). Ceramic tiles

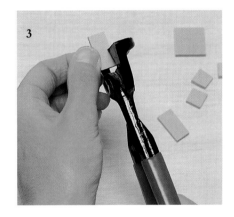

can be cut into quite small pieces just as long as you can hold the tile.

Cutting triangles

● It is quite difficult to cut accurate triangles with tile nippers. Hold the ceramic tile firmly and angle the nippers to cut diagonally across the tile (**5**). Squeeze gently. Cutting triangles takes practice, but you should always keep unsuccessful attempts, as they can be used elsewhere in the design.

● To trim the triangle, hold the tile nippers along the edge you want to trim. Snip off a little at a time until the edge is straight. If you try to cut too much at once, the tile will shatter.

● It is often much easier to use a glass cutter for cutting triangles than to use tile nippers. Use the scoring wheel to score across a glass tile. There is no need to go right from edge to edge, but you need to press hard to make a deep score with one movement; working backward and forward over and over again will produce a less accurate break.

● Insert the tile into the jaws of the cutter, aligning the score with the marker at the front of the tool (**6**). Press the jaws firmly to snap the tile. If you are too gentle, the tile is likely to crumble at the corners.

Cutting curves

● Simple curves and more complex shapes can be cut using tile nippers. It helps to draw the shape on the tile before beginning. Ceramic tiles in particular will break in a short curve if you hold the nippers at an angle near one corner (**7**). With practice you will be able to create the same shape again and again.

● To create longer curves, mark the shape on the tile and make a series of cuts to "nibble" away until you achieve the desired shape.

Cutting circles

● Circles are useful for details such as flower centers and eyes and are not difficult to cut. Cut a square about the same size as the finished circle. Turn the nippers around so that you use the curved cutting side. Cut across each of the corners to make an octagon.

● Work around the octagon, nibbling off the points until you have created a rough circle (**8**). Continue working around the shape, nibbling away at the edge, to produce an accurate circle.

PLANNING THE MOSAIC

It is a good idea to lay the mosaic out on a flat template before transferring the pieces to the glass surface. This allows you to plan how you are going to cut the tiles and where the grout lines are going to flow. For the background, you can produce a feeling of movement by following the curved lines of the design or lay the tiles straight across to create a harmonious effect.

● Wrap a piece of layout paper around the container to ascertain the space you have to work on and cut the paper to size. Enlarge the chosen templates to the required size and arrange them underneath the paper on a flat surface. Move the templates around until you are happy with the arrangement, then trace the design onto the layout paper with a marker pen. Draw in any lines that are essential to the shape of the motif, such as the outline of petals or leaf veins.

● Lay out the tiles on the tracing, remembering to leave small gaps between them for grout. Cut the tiles accurately around the edge of motifs or along design

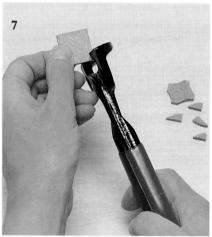

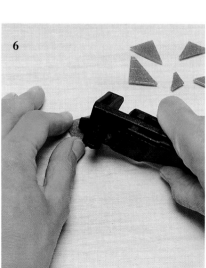

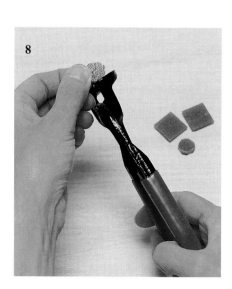

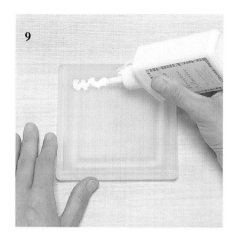

9

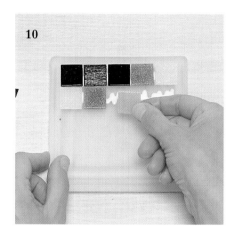

10

11

clear-drying glue. White school glue is ideal for sticking both glass and ceramic tiles to glass objects. Leave the glued mosaic for twenty-four hours before grouting.

● When you have planned your mosaic, transfer the design onto the glass by drawing around the cutout templates with an overhead projector pen.

● Squeeze the glue straight from the container or use an old paintbrush to apply it to a small area of the design marked on the glass at a time (**9**). Push whole or cut tiles onto the glue, remembering to leave gaps between the tiles, following your plan (**10**). Repeat until the whole area is covered. Leave for twenty-four hours to dry.

● To keep tiles from slipping on a curved surface, work in narrow bands and allow the glue to dry slightly before turning the container around (**11**).

GROUTING

Grout is the material that fills in the gaps between the tiles, giving a smooth finish and protecting the mosaic from water and dirt. Grouting pulls the elements of the mosaic together and draws attention to the layout. In general, you should choose a grout color that matches the colors in the mosaic. Buy powdered grout specially made for mosaic and add watercolor paint to change the color if desired.

● Prepare the grout according to the manufacturer's instructions. Fill a second container with water to have to sponge off the excess. How long the grout takes to dry will depend on the consistency of the mix, the surface it is used on, and the room temperature. As a rough guide, wait twenty to thirty minutes before sponging off the excess and twenty-four hours before scouring and polishing.

● Wearing protective gloves, spread the grout over the tiles using the back of a spoon or a grout spreader (**12**). Ensure all the gaps are filled by sweeping the spreader both horizontally and vertically.

lines to create a smooth grout line. This allows the eye to recognize the shape of the motif.

FIXING THE TILES

Most mosaic work is not designed to let light through, but when you are working on glass with vitreous glass tesserae, you can create a stained-glass effect by using a

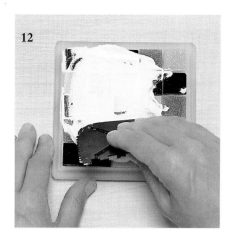

12

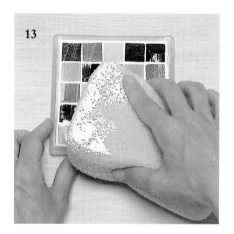

13

14

● After the grout has begun to set, wipe off the excess with a barely damp sponge (**13**). Keep rinsing the sponge, otherwise you will simply reapply the grout. Once clean, leave to dry.

● When the grout is completely dry, lightly scrub the tiles with a kitchen scouring sponge (**14**) and buff gently with a soft cloth.

The aluminum wire that is used in this funky candle holder is quite soft so that the coils can be bent and moved easily. It's surprising how much heat rises from even a tiny candle, so care must be taken to use a nonflammable material for the hanger. Simpler candle holders can be made from long twisted lengths of copper wire.

hanging candleholder

you will need
- safety glasses
- wire cutters
- 16 ft. of 16-gauge aluminum wire
- round-nosed pliers
- 131 ft. of 24-gauge copper wire
- flat-nosed pliers
- 6 ft. of 36-gauge copper wire
- glass candleholder

see also
Wirework, pages 12–13

● **SAFETY**
Never leave a lit candle unattended and always burn candles in a safe place away from drafts, soft furnishings, or any other flammable material, and out of the reach of children and pets.

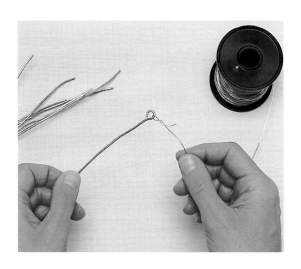

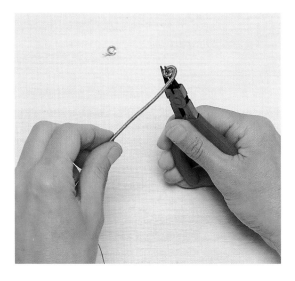

1 Wearing safety goggles, cut nine 2¾-in. lengths of 16-gauge aluminum wire. Using round-nosed pliers, make a small loop at one end of each length. Twist the end of a reel of 24-gauge copper wire around one loop and begin to closely wrap it around the aluminum wire, keeping the wrapping at the same angle.

2 Closely wrap 4–6 in. of the aluminum wire with copper wire, then cut off the loop of aluminum wire. Use round-nosed pliers to hold the end of the wrapped wire and bend it around to form an open coil. Continue turning the coil with the round-nosed pliers bending the wire around until you make a coil about ¾ in. in diameter.

3 Continue closely wrapping the rest of the aluminum wire with copper wire until the action becomes awkward. Turn the wrapped wire around and loosely coil the unwrapped end to make wrapping more manageable. Continue wrapping, opening the loosely coiled end out as needed. Trim the excess wire. Closely wrap and coil the ends of the other pieces of aluminum wire in the same way.

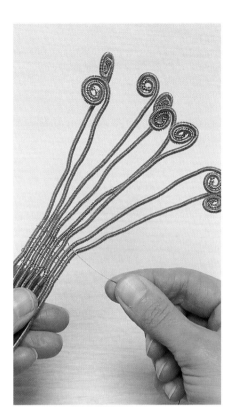

4 Take eight of the wrapped wires and make a roughly ¾-in. diameter open coil at their previously uncoiled ends. Hold them together 3–4 in. from one coil. Secure the end of a 3-ft. length of 36-gauge copper wire around a wrapped wire at one edge of the group. Weave the copper wire over and under each of the eight wrapped wires to secure them in a line. Weave back the other way just above the first line of weaving. Five or six lines of weaving should be enough to secure the wrapped wires together. Bring the two outside wires together to make a bundle and wrap the 36-gauge wire around a few times. Trim the excess copper wire and wrap it around one of the wrapped wires.

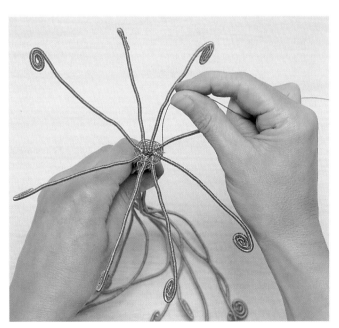

5 Pick the bundle up and bend the wires out above the weaving into a flat, circular star shape. Twist the end of a 3-ft. length of 24-gauge copper wire around the base of one of the uprights to secure it, and weave it over and under the wrapped wires about ten times to make a small circle of basketwork. Trim the excess wire and thread the end into the basketwork.

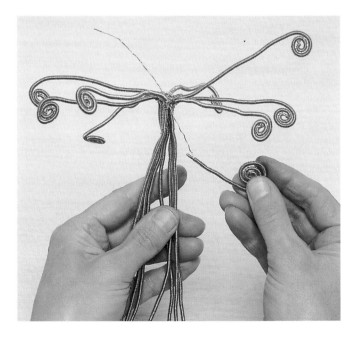

6 Cut the ninth length of wrapped wire about 2 in. from the coil. The other end will be used later. Unwrap some of the copper wire at the bottom and feed it into the center of the bundle of eight wrapped wires from below. Thread the wire through the basketwork to secure, and trim the excess wire close to the basketwork.

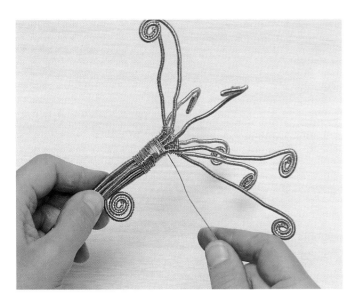

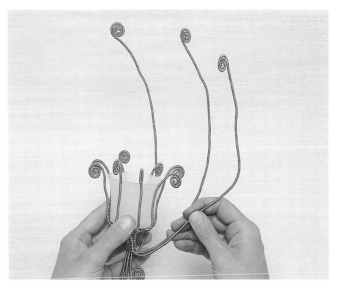

7 Hold the eight wrapped wires together with the shorter coil in the middle upside down. Wrap more 24-gauge copper wire around the stem of all nine wrapped wires for about ¾ in. and trim the excess. Thread the end back into the wrapping.

8 Hold a glass candleholder centrally over the basketwork and bend the wires up to hold it. Bend the other ends of the wires up and over the candleholder. Hold them about 3 in. from the top and wrap with 36-gauge copper wire to secure temporarily.

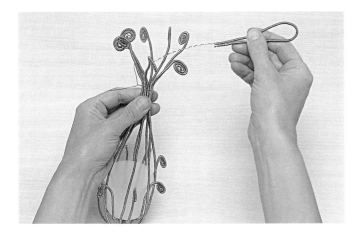

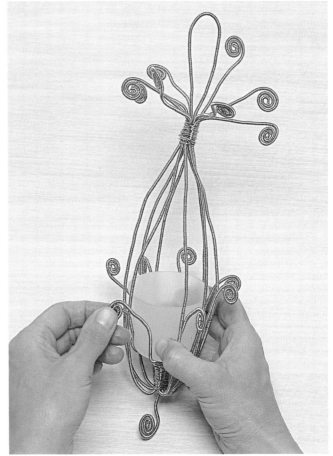

9 Take the wrapped wire put to one side in Step 6 and cut a 7-in. length from it. Bend it in half to make a loop. Unwind a length of the copper wire from one end and tuck it into the center of the wrapped wires from above. Wind the copper wire around the wrapped wires to secure the loop. Wrap 24-gauge copper wire around the eight wires and the loop for about 1 in. to secure.

10 Adjust all the wires to make sure they are equally spaced, smoothly curved, and pleasing to the eye.

Glass baking dishes are easy to use but can look rather unexciting. So why not make this stunning basket? Galvanized wire is a hard, noncorrosive wire that will hold its shape once bent to ensure that the hot dish is transferred from the oven to the table stylishly and safely.

oven-to-table dish basket

you will need
- safety glasses
- wire cutters
- 40 ft. of 20-gauge galvanized wire
- masking tape
- vise
- cup hook
- electric drill
- 40 ft. of 16-gauge galvanized wire
- cutting mat
- flat-nosed pliers
- 2-qt. oval casserole dish
- bowl
- 33 ft. of 30-gauge silver-plated wire
- ½-in. zinc-plated washers, 22

see also
Wirework, pages 12–13

1 Wearing safety glasses, cut a 20-ft. length of 20-gauge galvanized wire. Fold the wire in half and tape the ends together. Secure the taped ends in a vise. Fit a cup hook into the end of an electric drill. Loop the folded wire over the cup hook and walk back until the wire is fairly taut. Still wearing safety glasses and with the drill set on a slow speed, twist the wire until the twists are tightly packed. Reverse the drill for several turns to take the tension out of the wire, then unhook the loop and remove the tape from the ends.

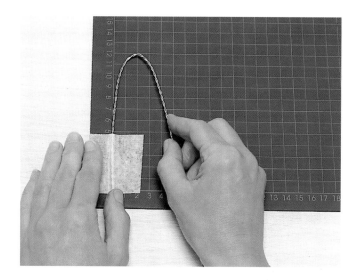

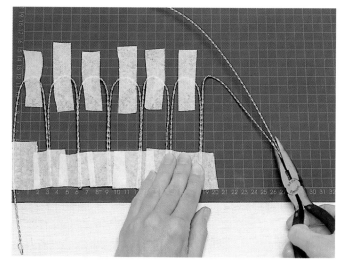

2 Repeat to make two twisted lengths of 20-gauge galvanized wire and two of 16-gauge galvanized wire. Tape one end of one of the thin wire twists to a cutting mat. Bend the wire into an upside-down U shape 1¼ in. wide and 4¾ in. high. The grid on the cutting mat makes a useful guide.

3 Use flat-nosed pliers to bend the end of the twisted wire back on itself and continue to make ten U shapes of the same height and width on the mat, taping the wire into position as you go. Trim at either end, level with the closely bent wire at the bottom of the U shapes. Make a second set of ten U shapes.

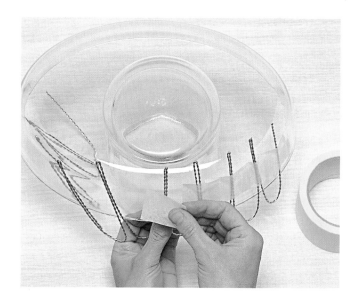

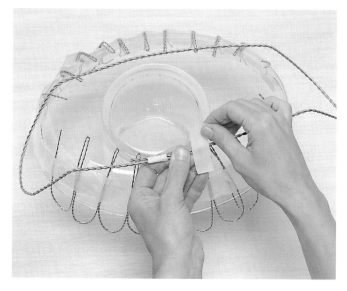

4 Position a 2-qt. oval casserole dish upside down over a bowl or other container that raises it slightly, making it easier to work around. Tape both lengths of shaped wire to the sides of the dish so that the loops hang down about ¾ in. below the rim of the dish and there is an equal gap at each end. Bend the ends to follow the shape of the dish.

5 To make the handles, cut one of the thicker pieces of twisted wire to a length of approximately 41 in. and form it into a long oval. Overlap the ends and secure them together with masking tape. Position the oval centrally on the bottom of the dish. Bend the ends down to create the handles. Release the tape from the overlapped ends and adjust the length of the oval as needed.

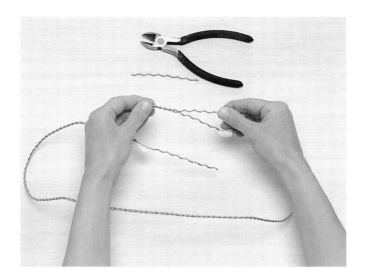

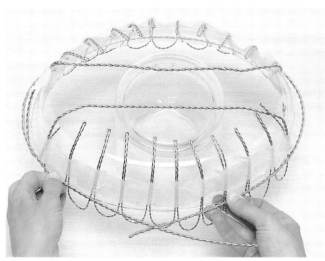

6 Use more tape to mark where the ends overlap. To join the ends of the handles, snip one of the twists next to the tape. Untwist and remove the cut piece. Cut one twist on the opposite wire next to the tape and untwist and remove the cut piece. Twist the two remaining pieces of wire back together to complete the oval. Tape the handle oval to the dish.

7 Cut a 37-in. length of thick twisted wire. Form it into an oval around the top of the dish, over the taped wire. Use tape to mark where the ends overlap. Join the ends as in Step 6 and tape the oval in position on the dish.

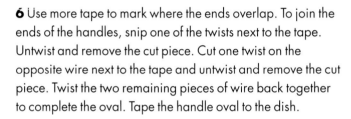

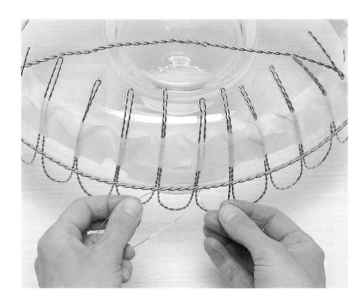

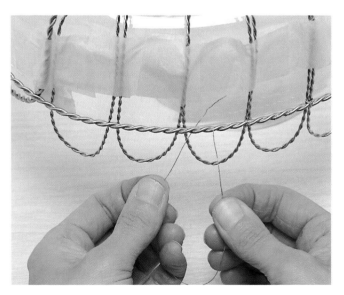

8 Halfway between the two handles on one side of the dish, thread the end of a manageable length of 30-gauge silver-plated wire under the twisted wires where a loop meets the oval on the rim. Pull the wire through so there are equal lengths on either side of the point where the two twisted wires meet. Wrap one end of the silver wire four times around the joint, then wrap it four times the other way to form a cross.

9 Wrap the silver wire along the horizontal wire until you reach the next upright. Cross the wire eight times over the joint. Continue securing the twisted wires tightly with silver wire until you reach the handle. Cross the handle, trim the excess wire, and tuck it out of sight. Repeat from where you began to the other handle, and on the other side of the dish. To join on further lengths of silver wire, twist together the end of a new wire and the end of the almost-finished wire at a cross and tuck them out of sight. Remove the masking tape.

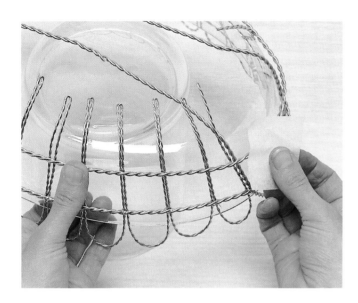

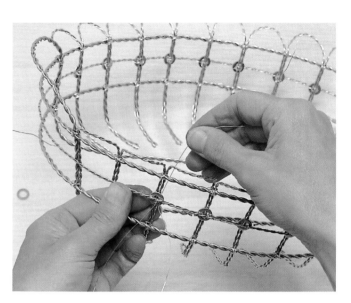

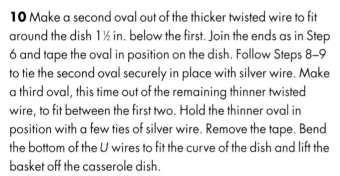

10 Make a second oval out of the thicker twisted wire to fit around the dish 1½ in. below the first. Join the ends as in Step 6 and tape the oval in position on the dish. Follow Steps 8–9 to tie the second oval securely in place with silver wire. Make a third oval, this time out of the remaining thinner twisted wire, to fit between the first two. Hold the thinner oval in position with a few ties of silver wire. Remove the tape. Bend the bottom of the U wires to fit the curve of the dish and lift the basket off the casserole dish.

11 Before tying crosses to secure the thin wire oval, tuck a zinc-plated washer between the horizontal and upright struts. Weave the fine wire through the washer and over the horizontal wire before taking it back across the upright. Repeat several times to secure the washer and the joint. Wrap the fine wire along the horizontal until you reach the next cross point, and continue in the same way. Trim the excess wire and tuck it out of sight.

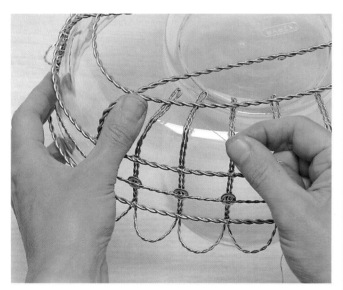

12 Place the basket back over the oven dish. Make a final oval from the thick twisted wire to fit over the bent ends of the U wires on the bottom of the dish. Tie each end to the oval with silver wire in a tight cross and make sure there are no loose ends that could scratch a table.

It doesn't take any special skills or tools to transform a plain glass decanter with finely woven wire. You can use aluminum wire, as here, or silver-plated wire for the coils, and choose one of the many stunning colors that are available in enameled copper wire to complete the weaving that surrounds the body.

wire-woven decanter

You will need
- safety glasses
- wire cutters
- 13 ft. of 16-gauge aluminum wire
- round-nosed pliers
- masking tape
- glass decanter, approximately 10 in. tall
- tape measure
- 30-gauge blue-enameled copper wire

see also
Wirework, pages 12–13

● TIP
How you weave the wire for this project will depend on the shape of the decanter. With this rounded shape, it was necessary to wrap the wire with the ridges to the inside, but a square decanter would probably work better if the ridges were on the outside.

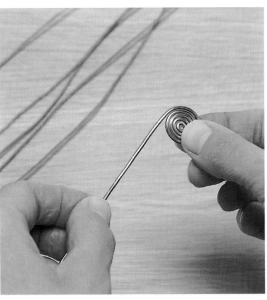

1 Wearing safety glasses, cut six 20-in. lengths of 16-gauge aluminum wire. If the wire is dull, it can be cleaned with metal polish and rubbed with a soft cloth until shiny. Use a pair of round-nosed pliers to make a small loop at the end of one length of aluminum wire.

2 Hold the loop between your thumb and forefinger and bend it around to form a closed coil. Continue bending the wire around until the coil has a diameter of about ¾ in. Repeat on the remaining lengths of aluminum wire. Avoid using pliers, as they will dent the soft wire.

3 Use masking tape to fix two of the lengths of wire opposite each other on either side of the decanter so that the coils are positioned about two thirds of the way up. Measure around the decanter and tape the remaining lengths of wire in position equally spaced between the first two.

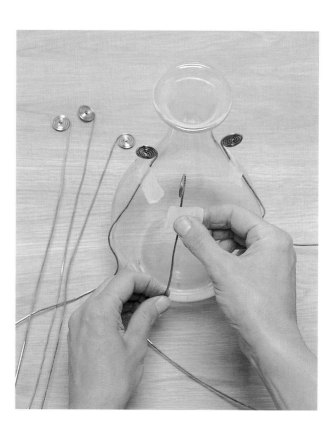

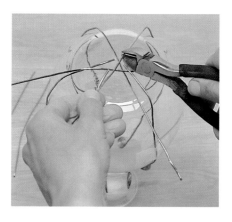

4 Turn the decanter upside down and bend the ends of the wires over the base. Trim the ends that overlap the base to about ¾ in. Use round-nosed pliers to bend the ends into small loops. Tape over the aluminum wires just under the halfway point on the body of the decanter. Remove the tape from two-thirds up the decanter.

5 Starting from the new tape lines and using 30-gauge blue-enameled copper wire directly from the reel, weave around the decanter, looping the blue wire once around each upright. Continue weaving around to the top of the aluminum wires to create a smooth, closely woven surface. Wind the end around an aluminum upright and trim the excess wire.

6 Remove the remaining tape and add pieces of tape around the top edge of the woven wire to hold it in place. Turn the decanter upside down. Weave more blue-enameled wire from where the first weaving began to the bottom of the decanter. Wind the end around an aluminum upright to secure and trim the excess wire.

Sometimes the simplest ideas are the best. Delicate twisted wire and flower-shaped metallized beads are all that are needed to decorate this pretty colored vase. To make a matching set, try to arrange the beads exactly the same distance apart on each wire and wind the wire in the same direction. Use a glue that is suitable for sticking beads to glass.

bead-and-wire-wrapped colored vase

You will need
- 5 ft. of 24-gauge silver-plated wire
- colored vase, approximately 8 in. tall
- ruler
- safety glasses
- wire cutters
- masking tape
- vise
- cup hook
- hand drill
- silver flower beads, $^5\!/_{16}$ in., approximately 20
- silver crimps, approximately 40
- flat-nosed pliers
- glue

see also
Wirework, pages 12–13
Beadwork, pages 14–15

1 Wrap the end of a reel of 24-gauge silver-plated wire around a glass vase and make a note of its length. Wearing safety glasses, cut the wire approximately two and a half times this length.

2 Fold the wire in half and tape the ends together with masking tape. Secure the taped ends in a vise. Fit a cup hook to a hand drill. Slip the folded loop over the cup hook and walk back until the wire is fairly taut. Wearing safety glasses, turn the drill to twist the wire. Reverse the drill for several turns to take the tension out of the wire.

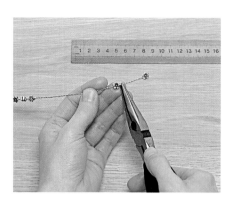

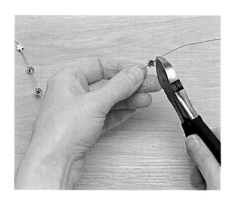

3 Carefully unhook the loop from the cup hook and cut the masking tape from the other end of the wire. Thread a silver flower bead onto the twisted wire from the cut end, followed by two crimps and another flower bead. Thread on approximately twenty flower beads with two crimps between each.

4 Bend the wire at the cut end over the first bead and cut off the excess. Use flat-nosed pliers to squeeze the first crimp to hold the bead in position. Move ¾ in. along the wire and squeeze the next crimp. Push the second bead into position and squeeze the crimp on the other side of the bead.

5 Continue squeezing crimps until all the beads are held in place, ¾ in. apart. Bend the wire over the last bead and trim the excess.

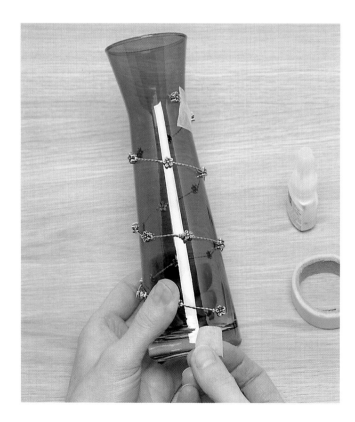

6 Wrap the beaded wire around the vase and hold it in place with masking tape at either end, just on the inside of the end bead. Lift up the end beads and fix in place with strong glue. Leave the tape in place until the glue dries.

● **SAFETY**
Remember to always wear safety glasses when twisting wire, since wire has a tendency to snap if the tension is too high.

Glass oil lamps provide an attractive way of creating subtle lighting, indoors or out.

For a special occasion, use colored oil and decorate the lamp with some beautiful crystal

beads that complement the color of the oil. When lit, the beads will twinkle in the soft

light and look quite stunning.

beaded oil lamp

you will need
- 8 in. of 19-gauge silver-plated wire
- glass oil lamp, approximately 7 in. tall
- tape measure
- safety glasses
- wire cutters
- round-nosed pliers
- 164 ft. of 30-gauge silver-plated wire
- clear crystal beads, ³⁄₁₆–³⁄₈ in., approximately 60
- amber crystal beads, ³⁄₁₆–³⁄₈ in., approximately 60
- 164 ft. of 30-gauge copper wire

see also
Wirework, pages 12–13
Beadwork, pages 14–15

 TIP
You may prefer to thread all the beads onto the stem wire before you begin wrapping, remembering to alternate the colors.

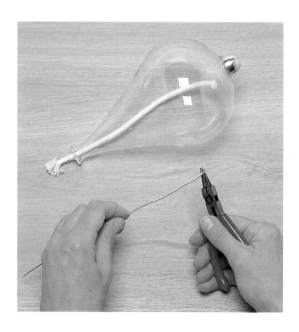

1 Wrap some 19-gauge silver-plated wire in a ring around the top of a glass oil lamp to find the required length of cut wire. Wearing safety glasses, cut the wire 2 in. longer than measured. Use round-nosed pliers to form a loop at one end of the wire.

2 Measure the height of the lamp to find the maximum length of wire stem needed. Twist the end of a 16-ft. length of 30-gauge silver-plated wire onto the loop of the core wire and closely wrap it along a few inches of the thicker wire, keeping the wrapping at the same angle. Pull the wrapping wire out to the side and thread on a clear crystal bead.

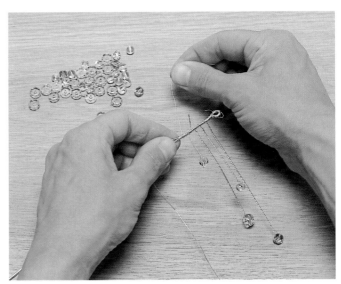

3 Hold the bead on the wire about as far out as the longest measurement taken in Step 2. Fold the thinner wire back on itself and wrap it around the core wire twice. Hold the bead between your finger and thumb, and twist so that the bent wire winds around itself to create a stem.

4 Pull the wrapping wire out on the same side of the core wire as before and thread on an amber crystal bead. Hold the bead on the wire, this time closer to the core wire, and bend and twist to secure on a stem. Continue along the length of the thick wire, alternating between clear and amber beads and choosing random lengths of stem until you have used approximately half the beads. Join on extra wire as needed.

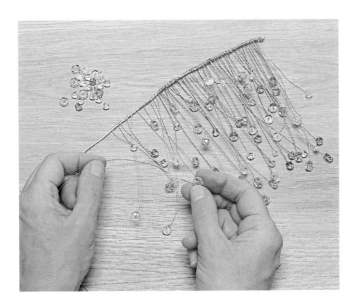

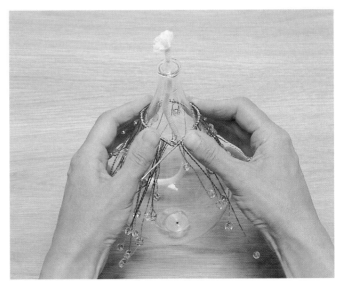

5 Twist the end of a 16-ft. length of 30-gauge copper wire onto the loop of the core wire and repeat Steps 2–4, adding a bead on a twisted stem between each silver-plated stem. Alternate the lengths of the stems as before. Trim the excess silver and copper wires and wrap them around the core wire.

6 Bend the finished beaded wire around the oil lamp. If necessary, push the beaded stems along the wire to fit. Use the round-nosed pliers to make a loop at the other end of the core wire where the two ends meet. Trim the excess core wire. Use the pliers to open one loop and hook the two loops together. Use the pliers to close the loop again. Bend the wire stems as necessary to create the finished look.

Available from selected florists, wire-mesh ribbon is an exciting new material that is an ideal base for beadwork. The beads can be added in a variety of ways, depending on the effect you are looking for. For the best results, use a wire that is the same thickness as the wire used to make the mesh to attach the beads.

decorated glass dish

you will need

- 3 ft. of wire-mesh ribbon
- straight-sided glass dish, approximately 4 in. tall
- ruler
- scissors
- safety goggles
- wire cutters
- 66 ft. of 36-gauge silver-plated wire
- metal beads, ¼-⅜ in., approximately 30 of each type
- light sapphire crystal beads, ³⁄₁₆ in. and ¼ in., approximately 50 of each
- sapphire crystal beads, ¼ in., approximately 100
- silver beads, ⅛ in., approximately 100
- 6 in. of 30-gauge silver-plated wire

see also
Beadwork, pages 14–15

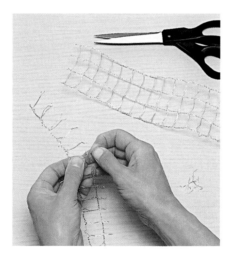

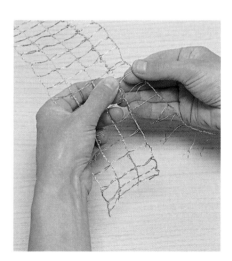

1 To make a strip of wire-mesh ribbon that is wide enough to cover the glass dish, you may need to join two pieces. Wrap some wire-mesh ribbon around the dish to find the required length and add on about 2 in. Use scissors to cut two pieces of mesh to this length. If you do not need the full width of one of the pieces of mesh, cut off the necessary number of extra rows directly underneath the horizontal strip of wire. Snip into the center of each square and pull the excess horizontal wire away gently.

2 Line the cut wires up with the squares on the first length of mesh ribbon. Twist the cut wire ends around the mesh to form a new row of squares, ensuring the squares are the same size as the other squares on the mesh. The wire and beads added later will help to strengthen this joint.

● **TIP**
To speed up the process of adding the metal or crystal beads, you can work along the mesh ribbon in a zigzag line.

3 Wearing safety glasses, cut a 3-ft. length of 36-gauge silver-plated wire and fold it in half. Tuck the bent end over the top corner of the mesh ribbon and twist the wire around the horizontal wire between the first and second squares to secure. At the first corner of the second square, thread a metal bead onto the doubled silver wire.

4 Twist the doubled wire around the top corner of the third square and adjust the length so that the bead hangs in the center of the second square of mesh. Wind the double wire down the side of the square and then thread the wire back through the bead. Twist the wire around the bottom corner to hold the bead securely in the center of the mesh square.

5 Attach metal beads in every second square of the mesh in a checked pattern, using at least two different-size beads randomly along the mesh. Wind the doubled wire down or across the mesh in preparation for attaching the bead to the next corner.

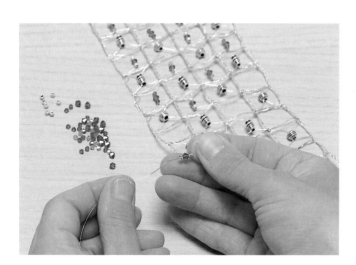

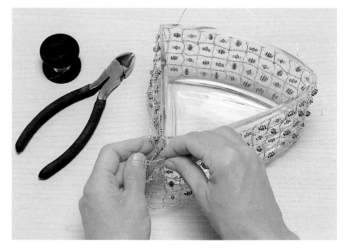

6 Cut a 3-ft. length of 36-gauge silver-plated wire and twist the end around the top corner of an empty mesh square. Feed on a small, large, then another small crystal bead. Wrap the wire around the opposite corner to make a loop that suspends the beads in the center of the square. Wind the wire down the side, back through the beads, and around the opposite corner to complete the loop. Work along the mesh, alternating shades of crystal beads and sometimes substituting small crystal beads with small silver beads. Trim the excess silver wires and twist them into the mesh to secure.

7 Wrap the mesh ribbon around the glass dish. Pinch the top edge of the mesh to mark each corner of the dish and then lie it out flat, ready to make corner hooks. Cut three 2-in. lengths of 30-gauge silver-plated wire and fold them in half. Hold the folded end ⅝ in. above each corner and wrap the cut ends along the top edge of the mesh ribbon to secure. Tie the ends of the mesh ribbon together with 36-gauge silver-plated wire and trim off the excess mesh. Fit the tied mesh ribbon shape over the glass dish and fold the hooks over the dish to hold it in position.

There is nothing quite as nostalgic as having real glass ornaments to hang on the tree at Christmas. Here are several ideas for decorating plain glass ornaments in a unique style using wire and beads. Rather than keeping with tradition, choose bright, modern colors and use silver wire to add a festive touch.

christmas ornaments

coiled wire ornament

you will need

- short length of spare wire
- clear glass ornament
- newspaper
- dust mask
- glass frosting spray
- safety glasses
- wire cutters
- 20 ft. of 19-gauge silver-plated wire
- flat-nosed pliers
- round-nosed pliers
- parallel pliers
- 20 ft. of 36-gauge silver-plated wire

see also
Wirework, pages 12–13

● **TIP**
The thickness of wire you choose will depend on the size of the ornament and whether you want a chunky or delicate look.

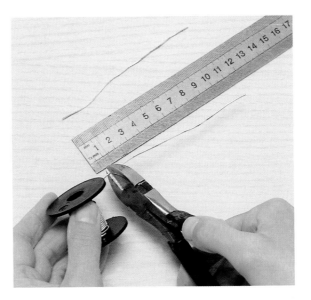

1 Tie a spare length of any wire through the loop at the top of a clear glass ornament so that it can be held and rotated. Wearing a dust mask and working in a well-ventilated area, test out the glass frosting spray on some newspaper, following the manufacturer's instructions, until you are comfortable with the coverage. Spray the glass ornament with a single coat of frosting.

2 Wearing safety glasses, cut 19-gauge silver-plated wire into 4¼-in. lengths. Cut the same number of 4-in. lengths for the S shapes. You will need at least twenty-five for the hearts.

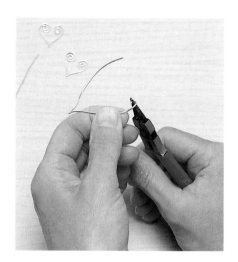

3 To make a heart shape, bend a length of wire in half and pinch the folded end with flat-nosed pliers. Shape the sides of the heart by curving the wire gently over the back of your thumb. Use round-nosed pliers to make a small loop at one end of the wire facing into the heart shape.

4 Hold the loop between the jaws of parallel pliers and bend it around to form an open coil. Continue turning the coil in the pliers and bending the wire to make a coil that has a diameter of about ⅜ in. Make a similar coil, facing in the opposite direction, on the other end.

5 To make an S shape, form an open coil at each end of a 4-in. length of wire, facing them in opposite directions. Make about twenty-five hearts and twenty-five S shapes.

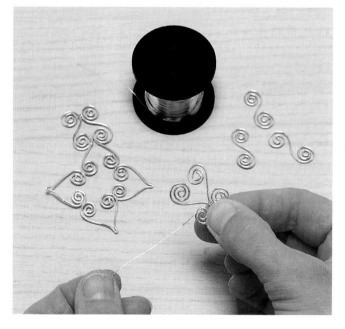

6 Take two heart shapes and wrap 36-gauge silver-plated wire around the outside of the coils four or five times to join them. Twist the ends together using flat-nosed pliers and trim to ⅛ in. Join four hearts together in the same way to form a circle.

7 Join a pair of S shapes together at one end, then join a pair to each of the four points of the hearts circle.

These small glasses are very popular and make pretty candleholders or delightful little vases for miniature flowers. Basic florists' galvanized wire makes a wonderful contrast to the frosted finish of the glasses used here. You can leave each glass separate or join the coils together to make a larger decoration.

shot-glass holder

you will need
- safety glasses
- wire cutters
- 6 ft. of 19-gauge galvanized wire
- frosted shot glass
- round-nosed pliers
- flat-nosed pliers
- masking tape
- paintbrush
- liquid safety flux
- soldering iron
- 50/50 tin/lead solder

see also
Wirework, pages 12–13

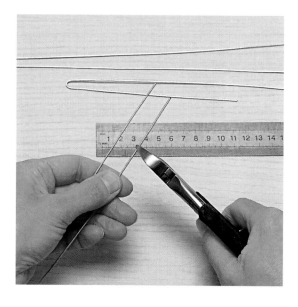

1 Wearing safety glasses, cut four 14-in. lengths of 19-gauge galvanized wire for one shot glass. Fold each wire in half and cut one end 1½ in. shorter than the other.

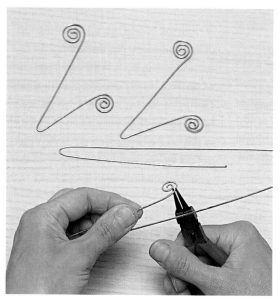

2 Use round-nosed pliers to make a small loop at the end of one wire. Hold the loop in round-nosed pliers and bend it around to form an open coil. Turn the coil in the pliers and bend the wire around until you make a coil with a diameter of about ⅝ in. Bend both ends of each wire into outward-facing open coils. Open the coils out to about sixty degrees.

3 To make a heart shape, bend a length of wire in half and pinch the folded end with flat-nosed pliers. Shape the sides of the heart by curving the wire gently over the back of your thumb. Use round-nosed pliers to make a small loop at one end of the wire facing into the heart shape.

4 Hold the loop between the jaws of parallel pliers and bend it around to form an open coil. Continue turning the coil in the pliers and bending the wire to make a coil that has a diameter of about ⅜ in. Make a similar coil, facing in the opposite direction, on the other end.

5 To make an S shape, form an open coil at each end of a 4-in. length of wire, facing them in opposite directions. Make about twenty-five hearts and twenty-five S shapes.

6 Take two heart shapes and wrap 36-gauge silver-plated wire around the outside of the coils four or five times to join them. Twist the ends together using flat-nosed pliers and trim to ⅛ in. Join four hearts together in the same way to form a circle.

7 Join a pair of S shapes together at one end, then join a pair to each of the four points of the hearts circle.

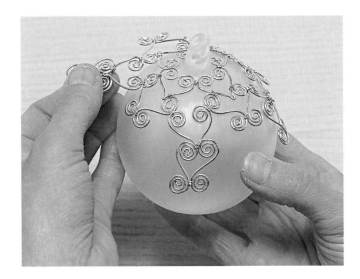

8 Drape the beginnings of the wired framework over the top of the ornament and check the positioning of the wires. Working on a flat surface, add other hearts and S shapes until the framework comes about halfway down the ornament.

9 Make the same arrangement of coiled wire pieces for the other side of the ornament. Tie the two wirework pieces together as much as possible off the ornament. Ease the ornament inside the wire covering, then tie off the few remaining joints and trim the wires.

beaded ornament

you will need

- short length of spare wire
- clear glass ornament
- newspaper
- dust mask
- glass frosting spray
- red seed beads, size 8/0, approximately 50
- 66 ft. of 36-gauge silver-plated wire
- masking tape
- vise
- cup hook
- hand drill
- safety glasses
- wire cutters

see also
Wirework, pages 12–13

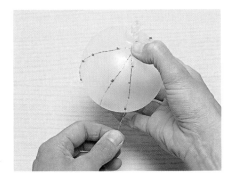

1 Follow Step 1 of Coiled Wire Ornament (see page 39) to frost a clear glass ornament. Thread about fifty red seed beads onto a 20-ft. length of 36-gauge silver-plated wire. Fold the wire in half and tape the ends together. Secure the taped ends in a vise. Fit a cup hook to a hand drill. Loop the bent wire over the cup hook and walk back until the wire is fairly taut. Wearing safety glasses, twist the wire to trap individual beads every few inches. Reverse the drill for several turns to take the tension out of the wire and unhook the loop.

2 Hold the end of the wire and begin to wrap it around the ornament. The first few turns are the most difficult because the wire has a tendency to slip off the ornament; once you get going, the beads will hold the wire in position. Keep wrapping until the whole ornament is evenly covered. Tie on a single thickness of 36-gauge wire and wrap around the ornament until the required coverage is achieved. Tie off the end and trim.

spring ornament

you will need

- short length of spare wire
- clear glass ornament
- newspaper
- dust mask
- glass frosting spray
- 82 ft. of 30-gauge colored, enameled copper wire
- size 8 knitting needle
- safety glasses
- wire cutters

see also
Wirework, pages 12–13

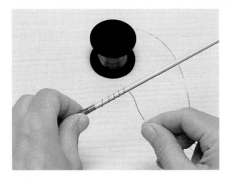

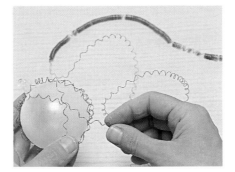

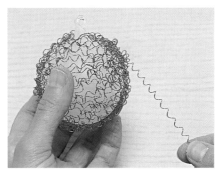

1 Follow Step 1 of Coiled Wire Ornament (see page 39) to frost a clear glass ornament. Wrap a length of the 30-gauge colored, enameled copper wire around a size 8 knitting needle, keeping the wire closely wrapped, until it is filled from one end to the other. Slip the tight spring off and continue winding to fill the needle again. Cut the wire at the end of the spring.

2 Hold the end of the spring at the top of the ornament. Pull the spring out to make a loose, curly wire and begin to wrap it randomly around the ornament. The first few turns are the most difficult because the curly wire has a tendency to slip off the ornament, but once you get going the curls will start to hold the wire in position.

3 Keep wrapping until the whole ornament is evenly covered. Trim the excess wire and twist the ends together for a neat finish.

These small glasses are very popular and make pretty candleholders or delightful little vases for miniature flowers. Basic florists' galvanized wire makes a wonderful contrast to the frosted finish of the glasses used here. You can leave each glass separate or join the coils together to make a larger decoration.

shot–glass holder

you will need

- safety glasses
- wire cutters
- 6 ft. of 19-gauge galvanized wire
- frosted shot glass
- round-nosed pliers
- flat-nosed pliers
- masking tape
- paintbrush
- liquid safety flux
- soldering iron
- 50/50 tin/lead solder

see also
Wirework, pages 12–13

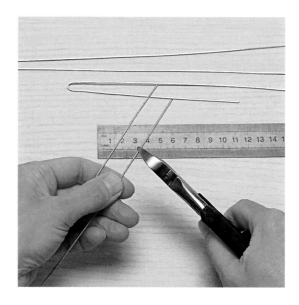

1 Wearing safety glasses, cut four 14-in. lengths of 19-gauge galvanized wire for one shot glass. Fold each wire in half and cut one end 1½ in. shorter than the other.

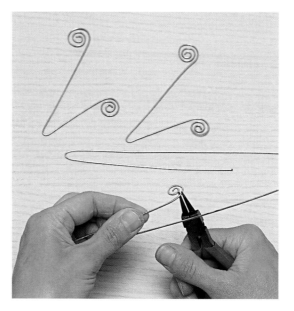

2 Use round-nosed pliers to make a small loop at the end of one wire. Hold the loop in round-nosed pliers and bend it around to form an open coil. Turn the coil in the pliers and bend the wire around until you make a coil with a diameter of about ⅝ in. Bend both ends of each wire into outward-facing open coils. Open the coils out to about sixty degrees.

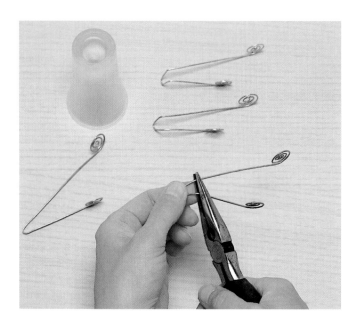

3 Use flat-nosed pliers to bend each wire about ½ in. from the fold. How much you bend the wire depends on the diameter of the base of your shot glass. The bent ends of four wires should butt together underneath the glass.

4 Wrap another length of galvanized wire around a shot glass at least twice and lift off. Cut the two curved lengths of wire about ½ in. longer than the full circle.

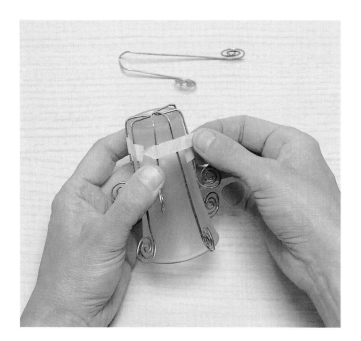

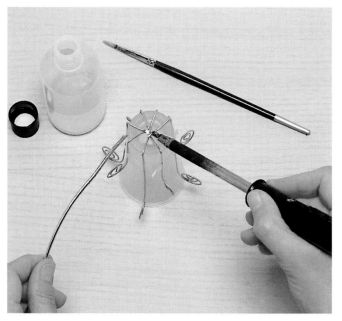

5 Turn the shot glass upside down and arrange the four wires with coiled ends around the glass so the bent ends meet underneath it. Alter the angle of the bent wires as needed and use masking tape at the side of the glass to fix the wires in the required position.

6 Following the manufacturer's instructions, use a paintbrush to paint a little liquid flux where the bent wires meet under the base of the glass. Heat the wires with a soldering iron and apply a little solder to fuse them together. Allow to cool.

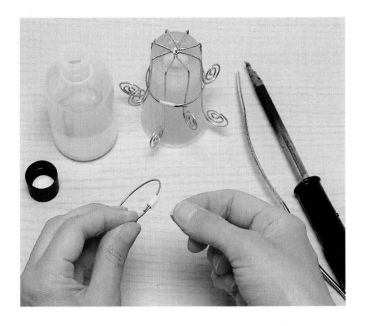

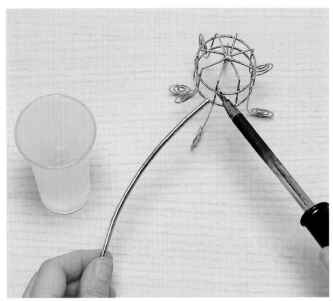

7 Remove the tape and bend in the side-coiled wires to follow the shape of the shot glass. Position the two circles of wire around the shot glass and side wires at the heights required and join the overlap close to the ends with masking tape. Follow Step 6 to solder together the circle joints, then remove the tape and trim the ends of the wire.

8 Fit the circles onto the shot-glass basket. Remove the glass from the basket and solder the points where the circles meet the side wires.

● **TIP**

The frosted finish on the shot glasses can be damaged by the heat of the wire as it is being soldered, so buy an extra glass to work on that can be thrown away once the project is complete.

Wire mesh is so pliable that it can easily be molded around any vase shape. The metal grid

makes an ideal base for beads, and its uniformity adds an elegant touch to the finished design.

Although any bead can be used, look for pretty ceramic beads in subtle, harmonious colors.

beaded tulip vase

you will need

- protective gloves
- tulip vase, approximately 8 in. tall
- 1 sheet of ¼ in. expandable, diamond wire mesh
- scissors
- 49 ft. of 30-gauge silver-plated wire
- ceramic ring beads, mixed colors, ¼ in., approximately 750
- flat-nosed pliers
- wire cutters
- safety glasses

see also
Beadwork, pages 14–15

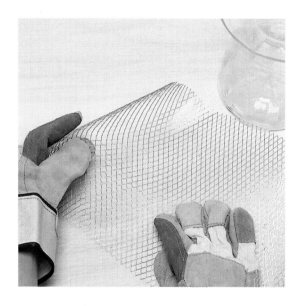

1 Wearing protective gloves, open out a sheet of expandable, diamond-wire mesh and pull to make wide diamonds along the bottom third of the mesh.

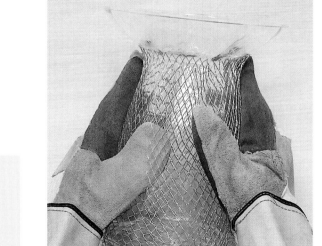

2 Wrap the mesh around the tulip vase and line the top edge of the mesh under the lip of the vase. Use your hands to ease the mesh into the shape of the vase. Make sure the grid holes remain evenly sized around the widest part of the vase, gradually getting smaller as the vase narrows.

● **TIP**
All sorts of beads can be used for this project, as long as they are washable (so that the vase can be cleaned after use).

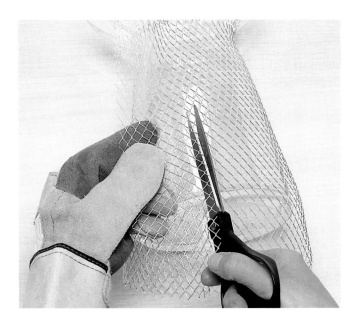

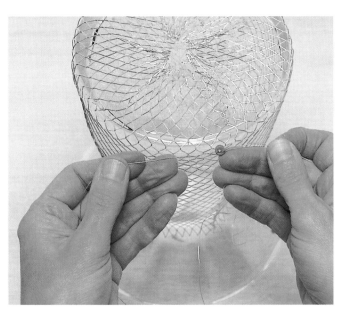

3 Where the mesh overlaps, trim it along the edge of one row of diamonds with scissors. Trim the other edge so that the mesh butts together in a straight line. Tie the joint together with a few short lengths of 30-gauge silver-plated wire and bend the excess under the base of the vase.

4 Turn the vase upside down and begin to add ceramic ring beads at the bottom of the vase, the widest part. At the joint between the two cut edges of the mesh, thread a manageable length of silver-plated wire under the mesh where it forms a cross, leaving a length of wire on each side. Thread a bead over both ends of the wire and push it down until it is resting over the cross. Open out the silver wire again.

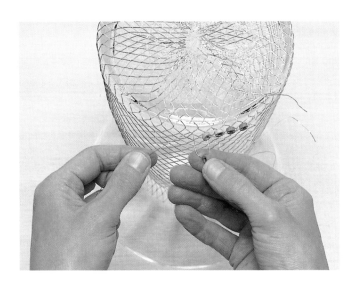

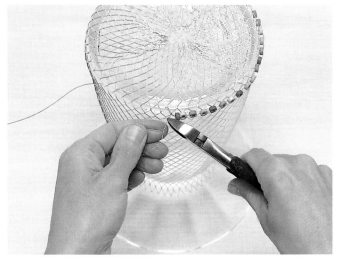

5 Thread another bead over the single length of wire on the other side of the bead, opposite the mesh joint. Loop the end of the wire under the cross on the mesh adjacent to the first and back through the bead. Continue around the vase, adding a bead at each cross.

6 When you come close to the end of the wire, join on another length. Thread the end of the new wire through the center of the bead and twist the ends of the new and old wires together. Twist the wire several times with flat-nosed pliers and trim close to the bead.

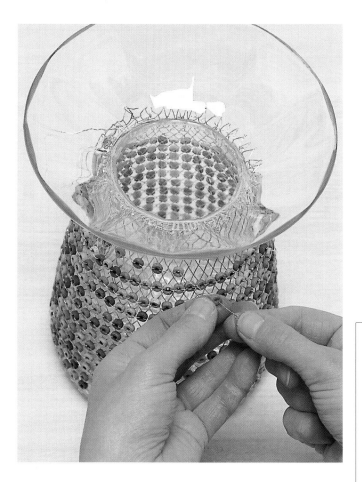

7 Continue adding beads, using a random selection of colors, until you get around to the joint again. Work your way up the vase, adding a row of beads at the top and bottom of each diamond. Turn the vase up the right way when it becomes difficult to work with it upside down. As the mesh narrows, the beads will be spaced more closely together. Once they touch all the way around, add beads only to every second cross.

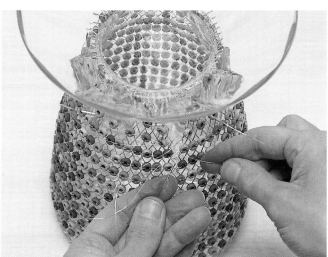

8 When you have covered the whole mesh with beads, lift off the beaded mesh carefully and clean the glass thoroughly. This will be the last chance you have to remove any fingerprints from the outside. Replace the mesh and twist all the silver wire ends together to secure the joint. Tuck the ends behind the closest bead and trim neatly. Trim the mesh on the base of the vase if necessary.

Pitchers remind me of wonderful alfresco meals on warm summer evenings, and the delicate string of beads on this glass pitcher catches the light as the sun goes down. Choose bead colors to suit your favorite drink, for example, red and gold for cranberry juice or bright yellow and silver for lemonade.

bead-decorated pitcher

you will need

- 6 ft. of 24-gauge gold-plated wire
- glass pitcher
- safety glasses
- wire cutters
- round-nosed pliers
- 16 ft. of 36-gauge brass wire
- red seed beads, size 8/0, approximately 100
- red square beads, ³⁄₁₆ in., approximately 40
- red round beads, ¼ in., approximately 40
- 2 red heart-shaped beads, ¾ in.
- masking tape
- strong glue

see also
Wirework, pages 12–13
Beadwork pages 14–15

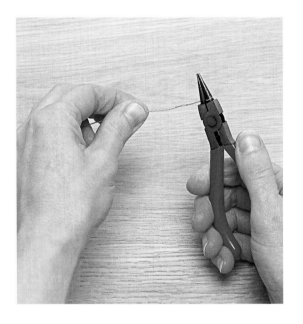

1 Wrap 24-gauge gold-plated wire around a glass pitcher several times, and wearing safety glasses, cut to the length required. Use a pair of round-nosed pliers to make a small loop at one end of the gold wire.

2 Twist the end of a 6-ft. length of 36-gauge brass wire onto the loop and closely wrap it along the first ¾–1¼ in. of the thicker wire, remembering to keep the wrapping at the same angle all along.

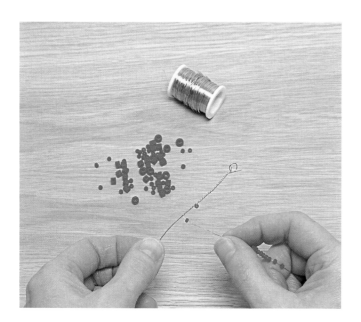

3 Pull the wrapping wire out to the side and thread on two seed beads, a square bead, and six more seed beads. Continue wrapping the brass wire around the core wire, trapping the first two seed beads about ½ in. apart.

4 Wrap for another ½ in., then pull the wrapping wire out to the side and hold the square bead about ½ in. away from the core wire. Fold the wrapping wire back on itself and wrap it around the core wire once or twice. Hold the bead between your finger and thumb, and twist so that the bent wrapping wire winds back around itself to create a secure stem.

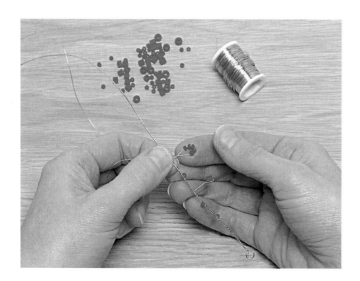

5 Continue to wrap the thinner wire around the core wire, trapping another seed bead on the core about ½ in. from the square bead stem. Wrap another ½ in. of core wire. Hold the next five seed beads about ½ in. away from the core. Bend the wire back on itself, wrap it around the core once or twice, and twist the beads to make a stem.

6 To make a small cluster of beads stand out from the core wire, thread on a seed bead, followed by a round or square bead, and finish with another seed bead. Bend the wire back on itself, leave the seed bead nearest to the bend, then thread the wire back through the round or square bead and the seed bead closest to the core wire. Pull the wire taut and continue to wrap the core wire.

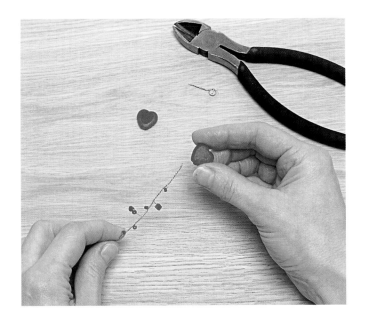

7 Follow Steps 3–6, adding individual beads, stems, and clusters in your preferred order. Keep the last ¾–1¼ in. of core wire free of beads. Snip off the wire loop at the other end, then thread a large heart-shaped bead onto each end. Bend each end of the wire over the top of each bead, then trim the excess.

8 Wrap the beaded wire around the pitcher and use masking tape to one side of each heart to fix the ends in position. Use strong glue to stick the hearts to the pitcher. Leave the tape in place until the glue is dry.

● **TIP**
If you decide to use a different type of bead, make sure you choose beads that will not be damaged when the pitcher is rinsed out after use. Beads with special finishes, such as imitation pearls, are not suitable.

Inspired by ivy growing up pillars, a pair of these beautiful candlesticks could grace the most elegant of dining tables. The rich burgundy, lilac, and green used here are very much winter colors, but you could use bright pastel beads for spring, or white and gold for a Christmas display.

candlestick with flower and leaf beads

you will need
- 3 ft. of 19-gauge burgundy-enameled copper wire
- glass pillar candlestick, 7 in. tall
- safety glasses
- wire cutters
- round-nosed pliers
- 8 ft. of 30-gauge burgundy-enameled copper wire
- lilac, pale green, and purple leaf beads, ½ in., 15 of each
- strong glue
- lilac and pale green flower beads, ½ in., 15 of each

see also
Wirework, pages 12–13
Beadwork, pages 14–15

● **NOTE**
To secure the flower heads to the wire, use a quick-setting glue that is suitable for sticking plastic to metal.

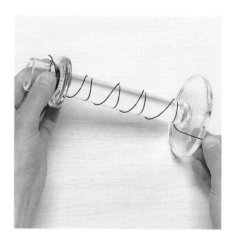

1 Wrap 19-gauge burgundy-enameled copper wire around a glass pillar candlestick. Wearing safety glasses, cut the wire to length, allowing a 2-in. excess. Take the wire off the candlestick and use round-nosed pliers to make a small loop at one end.

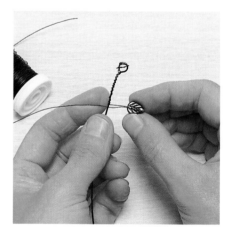

2 Twist the end of a 3-ft. length of 30-gauge burgundy-enameled copper wire onto the loop and closely wrap it along the first ¾–1¼ in. of the thicker wire. Pull the wrapping wire out to the side and thread on a leaf bead. Hold the leaf on the wire about ½ in. from the core wire. Fold the wrapping wire back on itself and wrap it around the core wire once or twice. Hold the bead between your finger and thumb and twist it so that the wrapping wire winds back around itself to create a stem.

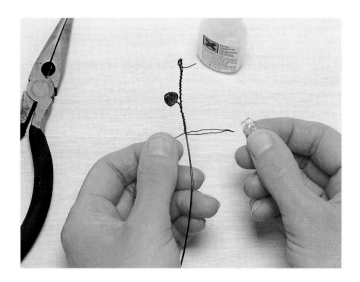

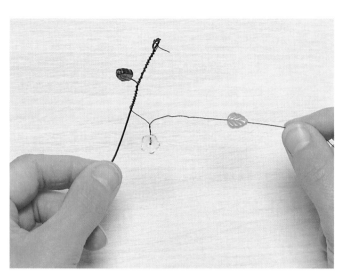

3 Continue to wrap the thin wire an additional ½ in. along the thick core wire. Pull the wrapping wire out to the opposite side from the leaf by about ¾ in. and fold it back on itself. Add a drop of strong glue to the fold and stick on a flower bead.

4 Once the glue has set, open out the bent wire and bend the flower bead down. Twist the bead so that the two lengths of wrapping wire wind around each other, but only wrap about half of the stem. Thread a leaf bead onto the wire about ½ in. from the flower, and bend and twist the wire as usual until this stem reaches the flower's stem.

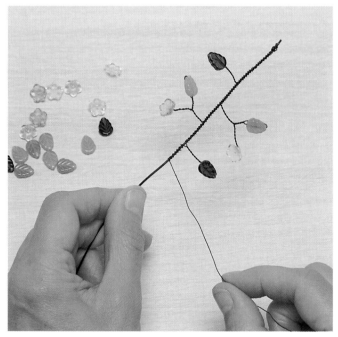

5 Hold both the flower and leaf beads between your finger and thumb, and twist them both to complete the stem back to the core wire.

6 Wrap the thin wire an additional ½ in. along the core wire. Alternating the colors of beads, make another flower and leaf stem on the opposite side, followed by a single leaf stem, again on the opposite side. Continue along the core wire making two flower and leaf stems, followed by a leaf stem until you reach the end.

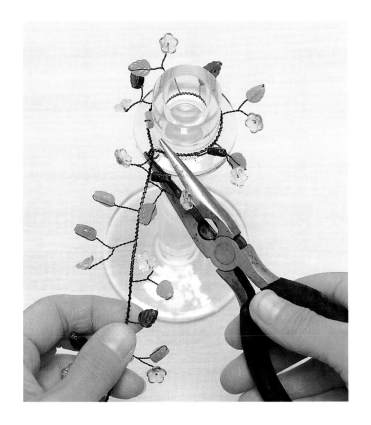

7 Starting at the looped end, wrap the beaded wire around the top of the candlestick. Open out the loop and hook it around the beaded wire where they meet. Close the loop again with pliers.

8 Wind the beaded wire down the pillar and once around the base. Make a loop with round-nosed pliers where the wires cross. Cut off the excess wire and open the loop out. Hook it over the beaded wire where the two meet and close the loop with the pliers.

● **TIP**
Once you have completed the wirework, carefully bend and arrange the leaves and flowers attractively so that they look as realistic as possible.

This simple mosaic mirror is an ideal project for the novice mosaicist. The special small vitreous glass tesserae make reasonably intricate designs possible without cutting. The larger ceramic tiles break the monotony and a careful choice of colors creates an ombré effect on the frame.

simple mosaic mirror

you will need

- ruler
- 10½-in. square of ½-in.-thick plywood
- marker pen
- 6-in.-square mirror tile
- adhesive fixing pads
- old paintbrush
- white school glue
- ½-in.-square vitreous glass mosaic tiles, approximately 100 each in ice, winter blue, pistachio, and pond green
- 1-in. glazed ceramic tiles, approximately 20 in porcelain white
- white grout
- red and green watercolor paints
- spoon
- protective gloves
- sponge
- scouring sponge
- soft cloth
- miter saw
- 47 in. of ¼ x 1-in. wood strip
- corner clamps
- masking tape
- cloth
- liming wax
- fine steel wool

see also
Mosaic, pages 15–17

1 Measure 2⅜ in. in from each edge of a 10½-in. square of ½-in.-thick plywood, and draw a square to mark the position of the mirror tile. Stick the mirror in place with adhesive fixing pads.

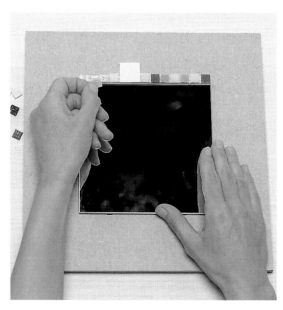

2 Use an old paintbrush to spread a line of white school glue along the top edge of the mirror tile. Stick a random mix of ½-in.-square vitreous glass mosaic tiles and a 1-in. glazed white ceramic tile along the top of the mirror, leaving a small gap between tiles for the grout.

3 Continue to apply small areas of glue and randomly mixed colored glass tiles up to the top of the plywood square. Try to gradually grade the overall color from light to dark as you work down the mirror frame by using predominantly ice and winter blue tiles at the top and slowly increasing the frequency of pistachio and pond green tiles at the bottom.

4 Fill the border around the whole mirror tile in the same way. Always start with the tiles along the edge of the mirror to ascertain the necessary spacing before completing the rest of the border. Leave for twenty-four hours to allow the glue to dry.

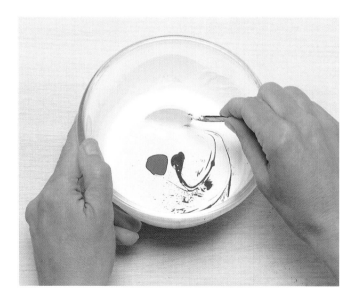

5 Mix white grout following the manufacturer's instructions and add a little red and green watercolor paint to color it to an off-white.

6 Wearing protective gloves, use the back of a spoon or a grout spreader to push the grout between the tiles, working horizontally and vertically to fill all the gaps. When the grout has just begun to set, wipe off the excess using a clean, damp sponge. Once the grout is completely dry, lightly scrub the tiles with a scouring sponge and polish with a soft cloth (see Grouting, page 17).

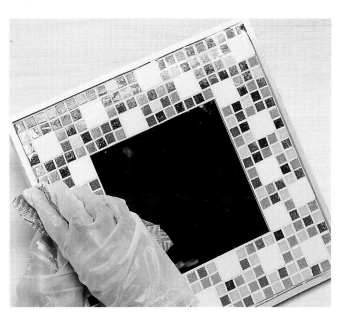

7 Use a miter saw to cut pieces of wood strip to fit around the sides of the mosaic frame and glue them into place. Use corner clamps and masking tape to hold the strips in place as the glue dries. Allow to dry for at least twenty-four hours.

8 Wear protective gloves and use a cloth to apply liming wax to the wood. Leave to dry, then rub with fine steel wool to remove the excess. Mix extra grout to fill the gap between the wood strips and the frame.

● **TIP**

Think about how you are going to hang the mirror before you begin. You can simply drill a hole in each of the top two corners of the plywood so that the mirror can be slotted onto two panel pins or you can attach a flush fitting to the reverse side.

If a glass dish has a chip, covering it with mosaic tiles can give it a new lease on life. The tulip design here requires quite a lot of tile cutting and arranging, so is not ideal for beginners. However, if you are new to mosaic, you could simply cover the dish in a mix of light and dark gray tiles.

mosaic dish

you will need

- tape measure
- glass dish, 12 in. in diameter
- overhead projector pen
- scissors
- ¾-in.-square vitreous glass mosaic tiles, approximately 20 each of dark orange, light orange, spring green, emerald green, dark olive green, dark red, light red, dark yellow, and light yellow; approximately 75 each of pale gray and medium gray
- safety glasses
- dust mask
- tile nippers
- glass cutter (optional)
- tweezers
- old paintbrush
- white school glue
- white grout
- black watercolor paint
- spoon
- protective gloves
- grout spreader (optional)
- sponge
- scouring sponge
- soft cloth
- spray matte varnish (optional)

see also
Mosaic, pages 15–17

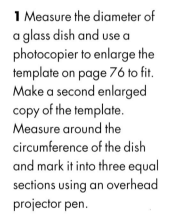

1 Measure the diameter of a glass dish and use a photocopier to enlarge the template on page 76 to fit. Make a second enlarged copy of the template. Measure around the circumference of the dish and mark it into three equal sections using an overhead projector pen.

2 Take one of the copied templates and cut out the tulip shapes. Position the templates inside the dish so that the base of each flower is level with one of the marks. Use masking tape to fix each tulip in place and the overhead projector pen to draw around the templates. Lift off the templates and draw the petal lines and parts of the stem covered by tape in freehand.

3 Wearing safety glasses and a dust mask, cut dark orange glass tesserae in half (see Cutting Techniques, page 15). Cut each of the rectangles in half to make four smaller squares. Place the spare template on a flat surface and arrange the quartered tiles on the main petal of a flower, leaving small gaps for grout. Use the nippers or a glass cutter to cut some of the quarter tiles into triangles to fit the pointed parts of the petals, and cut curves where necessary. Continue cutting and shaping the tiles to fill the main petal.

4 Complete the other petals using dark and light orange tiles. Use tweezers to position the smallest pieces. It is important to make the line around each petal as smooth as possible so that the tulip shape is quite distinct.

5 Use an old paintbrush to spread a thin layer of white school glue on the main tulip petal on the inside of the glass dish. Transfer the tiles to the dish following the plan. Check the spacing between the tiles. As the glue begins to dry, check that the mosaic pieces stay level and don't slip; if they do, carefully push them back into position.

6 Returning to the paper template, cut the quartered spring green tiles in half and use them to fill the stem. Use the quartered emerald and dark olive green tiles to fill in the main parts of the leaves, then cut smaller pieces to fill in the gaps. Follow Step 5 to stick the tiles to the dish, then complete the remaining two tulips, using light and dark red and yellow tiles for each flower.

7 Cut six to eight pale and medium gray tiles in half. Hold the tile nippers at an angle so that the tiles are slightly shaped. Stick half tiles alternately with whole tiles all around the rim of the dish. Fill in the area between the rim and the tulips using quarter tiles where possible, then work with smaller, specially cut pieces.

8 Use the overhead projector pen to mark the center of the dish. Trim a circle from a pale gray tile and stick it in the center. Use pale and medium gray tiles randomly to cover the dish from the center to the tulips, again using quarter tiles where possible and filling gaps with smaller, specially cut pieces. Allow the glue to dry for at least twenty-four hours.

● **TIP**

If the mosaic pieces slip down the sides of your dish, you probably need to use a stronger gluing method. Use a thin layer of tile adhesive to bed in the pieces, then grout in the normal way.

9 Mix white grout following the manufacturer's instructions and add a little black watercolor paint to color it to a medium gray. Wearing protective gloves, use the back of a spoon or a grout spreader to push the grout between the tiles, working horizontally and vertically to fill all the gaps. When the grout has just begun to set, wipe off the excess with a clean, damp sponge. Once the grout is completely dry, lightly scrub the tiles with a scouring sponge and polish with a soft cloth (see Grouting, page 17). If you are going to use the dish for floating candles, spray with several coats of matte varnish to seal the grout.

Any lamp that is used outside in the evening will attract moths, the inspiration behind this project. Choose a glass container with straight sides at the bottom and an open neck that will give you easy access to the candle from the top. For an 8-in. lamp, you will need approximately thirty black tiles and twenty each of the other colors.

mosaic hurricane lamp

you will need
- layout paper
- glass hurricane lamp or vase
- scissors
- marker pen
- masking tape
- overhead projector pen
- 1-in.-square unglazed ceramic tiles, turquoise, old rose, pink, gray-green, gray, green, white, granite blue, blue-gray, blue, black
- safety glasses
- dust mask
- tile nippers
- tweezers
- towel
- old paintbrush
- white school glue
- grout
- black watercolor paint
- spoon
- protective gloves
- grout spreader (optional)
- sponge
- scouring sponge
- soft cloth

see also
Mosaic, pages 15–17

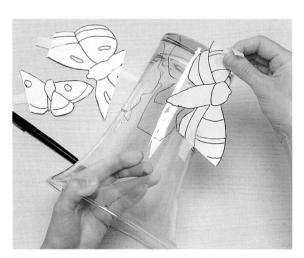

1 Wrap a piece of layout paper around the base of a hurricane lamp, mark the overlap, and cut the paper to the required length. Cut this strip 4 in. deep. Use a photocopier to enlarge the moth template on page 77 to the same depth. Place the photocopy under the layout paper strip and use a marker pen to trace the template.

2 Cut out the moths from the original template and use masking tape to fix them around the base of the hurricane lamp. Draw around the moth templates with an overhead projector pen, then remove the paper.

3 Use a range of gray, pink, old rose, turquoise, and black ceramic tesserae to fill in the first moth. Wearing safety glasses and a dust mask, cut each tile into small squares and rectangles (see Cutting Techniques, pages 15–16). Place the layout paper template on a flat surface and arrange the cut tiles on a moth, creating a similar pattern on each wing and leaving small gaps between the tiles for grout. The color of moths tends to be more muted than butterflies, but they still have similar patterns.

4 Cut circles or curves to fit the edges of the wings by cutting across each corner of a square and nibbling away until the shape becomes round.

5 Choose a slightly different color combination for the body of the moth so that it is distinct. To make the feelers, use the tile nippers to nibble small shards from the edge of a tile. You will need pieces that are thick enough to stand on their own but still fine enough to achieve the desired effect. Use tweezers to handle these tiny tiles.

6 Lay the lamp on a folded towel to balance it and use an old paintbrush to spread a thin layer of white school glue onto small areas of the first moth. Transfer the tiles to the lamp following the plan. Check the spacing between the tiles. As the glue begins to dry, check that the mosaic pieces stay level and don't slip. If they do, carefully push them back into position. The lamp has a curved surface, so you may need to wait a little while for the glue to dry before you can decorate the next area.

7 Return to the paper template to plan out each moth before sticking the tiles to the glass. Cut the black tiles into four pieces and then four again. Use these smaller black tiles to fill in the background, following the outline of the moths' wings and trimming the tiles to follow the curves where needed.

8 To neaten the top edge, stick a row of small black squares all around the top of the mosaic. Allow the glue to dry for at least twenty-four hours before grouting.

● **TIP**

When working on such a curved surface, it is essential that you only apply glue to small areas at a time and allow the glue to dry sufficiently before rotating the lamp to begin another section.

9 Mix white grout following the manufacturer's instructions and add a little black watercolor paint to color it to a dark gray. Wearing protective gloves, use the back of a spoon, a grout spreader, or your hands to push the grout between the tiles, working horizontally and vertically to fill all the gaps. When the grout has just begun to set, wipe off the excess using a clean, damp sponge. Once the grout is completely dry, lightly scrub the tiles with a scouring sponge and polish with a soft cloth.

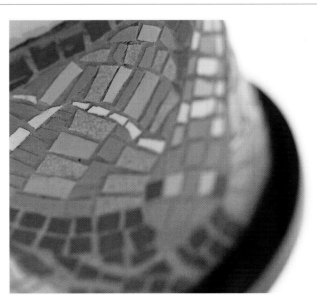

This rectangular vase has rounded corners, which means that the mosaic tiles cannot be attached directly to the glass with white school glue. Instead, the cut tiles are stuck upside down on heavyweight brown paper and pregrouted before the entire design is transferred to the vase.

rectangular vase

you will need

- ruler
- rectangular glass vase, 3 x 3 x 10 in.
- heavyweight brown paper
- marker pen
- scissors
- layout paper
- carbon paper
- white school glue
- old paintbrush
- ½-in.-square vitreous glass tiles, 150 ice, 40 winter blue, 100 pistachio, 200 moonlight blue, 60 pond green, 200 morning glory, 10 seal gray, 10 blue silk, 10 black
- safety glasses
- dust mask
- tile nippers
- plastic sheet
- white grout
- protective gloves
- grout spreader
- sponge
- cement-based adhesive
- ⅛-in. notched squeegee
- scouring sponge
- soft cloth

see also
Mosaic, pages 15–17

1 Measure the width and height of the sides of a rectangular glass vase and add ¼ in. to each measurement. Using these measurements, draw out four rectangular shapes on heavyweight brown paper and cut them out.

2 Use a photocopier to enlarge the leaf template on page 78 to fit the sides of the vase. Cut out layout paper to the same measurements as the brown paper and trace the template onto each strip of layout paper. Take a brown paper strip and cover with a sheet of carbon paper and a layout paper template. Draw back over the leaves on the layout paper to transfer the pattern to the brown paper. Repeat for each of the three remaining sides.

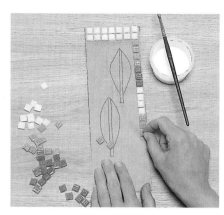

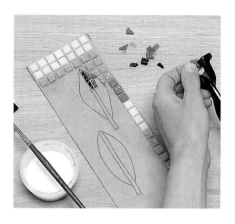

3 Lay a line of whole ice-white vitreous glass tiles upside down at the top of a brown paper strip with the beveled edge up. Adjust the spacing between tiles so that you do not need to use cut tiles at either end. Dilute white school glue 50:50 with water. Use an old paintbrush to apply the diluted glue to the area to be covered with ice tiles and fix the first rows in position.

4 Without gluing, arrange a row of ice, moonlight blue, and morning glory tiles down one side of the strip. Space them equally so that you do not need cut tiles at either end. When you are happy with the arrangement, glue the upside-down tiles in position.

5 Continue arranging and gluing whole tiles to fill the background. When you get close to the leaves, you need to cut the tiles to fit (see Cutting Techniques, pages 15–16). Use whole, quartered, and individually cut tiles in winter blue, pistachio, and pond green for the leaves. Complete all four panels similarly. Allow the glue to dry thoroughly. Check that all the tiles are stuck by lifting up the paper.

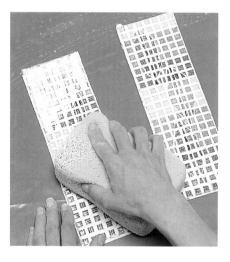

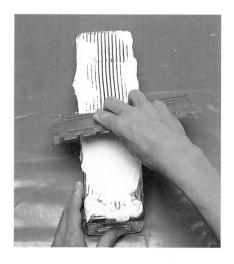

6 Protect your work surface with a waterproof covering, such as a plastic sheet. Mix white grout following the manufacturer's instructions. Wearing protective gloves, use a grout spreader to push the grout between the tiles on the paper, working horizontally and vertically to fill all the gaps.

7 When the grout has just begun to set, wipe off the excess with a clean, damp sponge. There must be no grout left on the back of the tiles or they will not stick properly to the adhesive in the next step. Grout all four paper strips and leave to dry.

8 Mix a cement-based adhesive following the manufacturer's instructions and use a ⅛-in. notched squeegee to apply it and spread it evenly over one side of the glass vase. The notches of the squeegee must touch the glass to ensure that the adhesive is spread evenly.

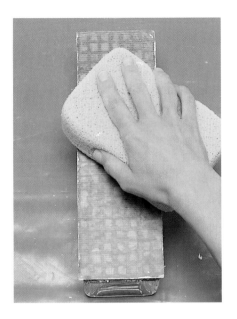

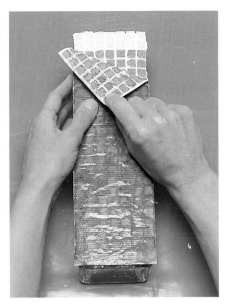

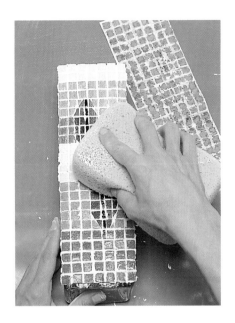

9 Lift one of the pregrouted mosaics on brown paper carefully onto the adhesive, paper-side up, making sure the edges of the paper and the vase line up. Press the paper down into the adhesive. Wet the paper with a clean, very wet sponge and leave for five to ten minutes to allow the paper to absorb the water.

10 Starting from one corner, peel back the paper to the middle of the panel. If the tiles along the edge come away, use your finger to stick them back down, making sure there is enough adhesive to keep them level. Move to the opposite end and peel the rest of the paper back to reveal the mosaic.

11 Use a damp sponge to clean the front of the mosaic. Follow Steps 8–11 for each side of the vase. If necessary, regrout the corners of the vase. Regrout the whole vase, including the corners and top rim. Once the grout is dry, lightly scrub the tiles with a scouring sponge and polish with a soft cloth to finish.

● **TIP**

Draw the design out on the matte side of the brown paper, as it is slightly more absorbent and will take the glue well.

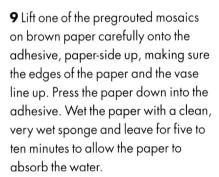

TEMPLATES

mosaic dish, p. 64

OVERLAP TEMPLATE ON THIS LINE

mosaic hurricane lamp, p. 68

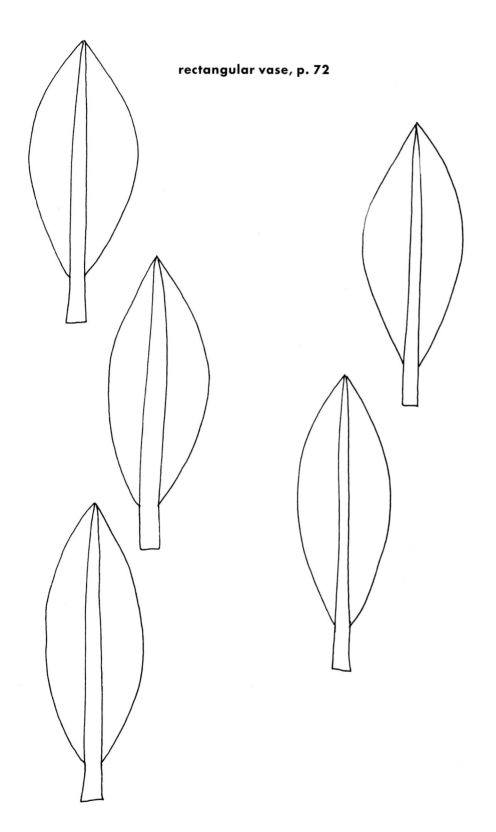

rectangular vase, p. 72

USEFUL
ADDRESSES AND SUPPLIERS

General

Artcity.com
1350 Kelton Ave., Ste.308
Los Angeles, CA 90024
(866) ARTCITY
www.artcity.com

Art Supply Warehouse
5325 Departure Dr.
Raleigh, NC 27616
(800) 995-6778
www.aswexpress.com

Jo-Ann Fabric & Crafts
5555 Darrow Rd.
Hudson, OH 44236
(800) 525-4951
www.joann.com

Lewiscraft
Yonge & Eglinton Centre
2300 Yonge Street
Toronto, ON M4P 1E4
(416) 482-6554
www.lewiscraft.com

Michaels
(800) MICHAELS
www.michaels.com

MisterArt.com
1800 Peachtree St. NW
Atlanta, GA 30309
(800) 423-7382
www.misterart.com

Texas Art Supply
2001 Montrose Blvd.
Houston, TX 77006
(713) 526-5221
www.texasart.com

Beads

Arizona Bead Company
957 E. Guadalupe Rd. B-3
Tempe, AZ 85283
(480) 491-4472
arizonabeadcompany.com

The Bead Gallery
3963 Main St.
Amherst, NY 14226
(716) 836-6775
www.bead gallery.com

Bead Need
6323 Stirling Rd.
Davie, FL 33314
(954) 791-1600
www.wenttopieces.com

Bead Warehouse
4 Meadowlake Dr.
Mendon , VT 05701
www.beadwarehouse.com

Beadworks
149 Water St.
Norwalk, CT 06854
(800) 232-3761
www.beadworks.com

Canada Beading Supply
200 Colonnade Rd. South
Nepean, ON K2E 7M1
(800) 291-6668
www.canbead.com

JewelArt
(818) 996-BEAD
www.jewelart.com

John Bead Corp. Ltd.
19 Bertrand Ave.
Toronto, ON M1L 2P3
(416) 757-3287
www.johnbead.com

The Place to Bead
2551 San Ramon Valley Blvd.
Suite #103
San Ramon, CA 94583
(925) 837-5544
www.placetobead.com

Mosaic

Mendel's and Far-Out Fabrics
1556 Haight St.
San Francisco, CA 94117
(415) 621-1287
www.mendels.com

Mosaic Mercantile, Inc.
P.O. Box 78206
San Francisco, CA 94107
(877) 9-MOSAIC
www.mosaicmercantile.com

Mosaic Tile Supply
10427 ½ Unit A Rush St.
South El Monte, CA 91733
(626) 279-7020
www.mosaicsupply.com

Mountaintop Mosaic,
P.O. Box 653
Castleton, VT 05735
(800) 564-4980
mountaintopmosaics.com

Olla Linda
7010-E Burnet Rd.
Austin, TX 78757
(512) 458-6422
www.importgallery.com

Wits End
5224 West SR 46
Sanford, FL 32771
(407) 323-9122
www.mosaic-witsend.com

Tools

Ace Hardware
2200 Kensington Ct.
Oak Brook, IL 60523-2100
(630) 990-6600
www.acehardware.com

Home Depot
2455 Paces Ferry Rd.
Atlanta, GA 30339
(800) 430-3376
www.homedepot.com

Lowe's Home Improvement
Warehouse
P.O. Box 1111
North Wilkesboro, NC 28656
(800) 44-LOWES
www.lowes.com

Paul Gesswein & Co. Ltd.
255 Hancock Ave.
Bridgeport, CT 06605
(203) 366-5400
www.gesswein.com

Wire

Highland Supply Corporation
1111 Sixth Street
Highland, IL 62249-0124
(800) 472-3645
www.highlandsupply.com

Metalliferous
34 West 46th St.
New York, NY 1003
(212) 944-0909
www.metalliferous.com

Paramount Wire Co.
2-8 Central Ave.
East Orange, NJ 07018
(973) 672-0500
www.parawire.com/craftstore

INDEX